FRED ASTAIRE

FRED ASTAIRE

A Pyramid Illustrated History of the Movies

by
STEPHEN HARVEY

General Editor: **TED SENNETT**

**PUBLICATIONS
NEW YORK**

For my family, but especially my mother—with love

FRED ASTAIRE
A Pyramid Illustrated History of the Movies

Pyramid edition published December 1975

ISBN 0-515-03870-9

Library of Congress Catalog Card Number: **75-39985**

Printed in the United States of America

Pyramid Books are published by Pyramid Communications, Inc. Its trademarks, consisting of the word "Pyramid" and the portrayal of a pyramid, are registered in the United States Patent Office.

Pyramid Communications, Inc., 919 Third Avenue, New York, N.Y. 10022

(graphic design by ANTHONY BASILE)

ACKNOWLEDGMENTS

I would like to express my thanks to many of my friends and colleagues for their aid and encouragement on this project, including Larry Mark, Gary Kalkin, Barbara Skluth, Vito Russo, Howard Mandelbaum, Ronnie Mandelbaum, Mary Corliss, Gary Carey, Emily Sieger, James Tamulis, Tony Yearwood, Susan Kemp, Diane Messer, Wendy Most, Linda Most, Albert Zwirn, and George Morris.

Pat Sheehan, Paul Spehr, and their co-workers at the Library of Congress Motion Picture Division as usual proved of invaluable assistance in my research, and the staff of the Lincoln Center Library for the Performing Arts was also most helpful. For their aid in obtaining prints, I would like to thank Wayne Hay of Willoughby-Peerless, and Budget Films. I am particularly indebted to Douglas Lemza of Films, Incorporated, in this regard; without his extraordinary cooperation, this book would not have been possible.

All of my colleagues at the Department of Film, Museum of Modern Art, have been amazingly forbearing and helpful during this time, and I am very grateful to them all.

Beth Genné generously contributed many valuable facts and insights, taking time away for her own projects to do so.

Richard Corliss' superb essay on screenwriters Betty Comden and Adolph Green from his book *Talking Pictures* is acknowledged in the bibliography that follows the text of this book, but I am in his debt for much more than that; as editor of *Film Comment* and as a friend, he has had an enormous influence on my work.

Finally, I am grateful most of all to Phillip Carlock, John Bohler, Charles Silver, and Bob Willis for their help on this book and their kindness and support at all times.

Photographs: Jerry Vermilye, The Memory Shop, Cinemabilia, Movie Star News, The Museum of Modern Art Film Stills Archive, and Quality First

CONTENTS

"I don't know how it started and I don't want to know. I have no desire to prove anything by it. I have never used it as an outlet or as a means of expressing myself.
I just dance."

—*Fred Astaire,*
from his autobiography,
Steps In Time.

INTRODUCTION: SHOES WITH WINGS ON

With these bland closing words from his autobiography, Astaire betrayed one of his most endearing and yet exasperating quirks as a performer—his utter bewilderment that anyone should take his work seriously. Although he merely managed to raise the movie musical from the level of empty spectacle to one of the few unquestioned glories of the American film, Astaire has always been notoriously sphinxlike about the nature of his art. One might just as well expect to see Garbo regaling the addicts of late-night television talk shows with charming anecdotes of her years at MGM, as Astaire shedding light on the internal motivations that have guided his work. Yet to accept Astaire's self-portrait as "just a dancer" would be as absurd as describing Chaplin as just a man who made people laugh, and leaving it at that.

Of course, Astaire largely owes his unassailable place in the pantheon of unique film stars to the agility of those famous feet. Well known for his tireless perfectionism, Astaire spent infinite hours planning, rehearsing, and reshaping each of those routines that always seemed so spontaneous and effortless onscreen. All this endless hard work gave Astaire his breathtaking craftsmanship as a dancer, and his vehement determination never to repeat himself showed off his matchless versatility. From film to film, Astaire mastered every conceivable style of dance, making them distinctively his in the process, from breathless tap solos to stately ballroom duets, from jitterbug to modern dance, even extending to classical ballet and ethnic folk motifs.

Yet mere dedication and expertise fail to explain why Astaire dominated the American film musical for a quarter century and remains one of the movies' few genuinely legendary figures. Talent alone has never guaranteed a sustained star career in films; numerous dancers with legs like pistons in swing time have briefly made their mark in films, only to find their fame waning as soon as the novelty of their style faded.

Ultimately they failed where Astaire succeeded because, like all Astaire's predecessors, they treated

With Adele Astaire in THE BAND WAGON (1931)

dance as a vaudeville specialty only slightly classier than the average canine balancing act, which served only as a fleeting diversion from the plots and actors that surrounded them. Astaire naturally excelled at this sort of routine, as he did at everything he attempted in the realm of musical comedy; such set pieces as the title number from *Top Hat* and "Puttin' On the Ritz" in *Blue Skies* are the most exhilarating examples imaginable of sheer joyous virtuosity on display. Yet Astaire's true achievement in movies was infinitely subtler and more revolutionary. Incredibly, he was the first to realize that dance could convey and even deepen any given emotion onscreen. When the movies evolved almost overnight from a silent to a sound medium, actors and filmmakers seemed to forget that the human voice was only one tool of their craft; consciously or not, Astaire reintroduced the heretical notion that the human body could express the deepest of feelings even without the benefit of words.

The peerless dance numbers that studded his series of films with Ginger Rogers don't just provide welcome relief from the transparent stories that surround them. Instead, Astaire's solos and his duets with Ginger give the plots resonance and feeling; they both comment on these paperweight tales and propel them forward.

Astaire doesn't merely tell us of Ginger's devastating effect on him—that would be too banal and too easy. Instead he sails over sofas and transforms prosaic objects like mantelpieces and seltzer bottles into syncopated instruments of poetry. In each of these films, a skeptical Ginger perpetually scoffs at Fred's gauche verbal passes in her direction; their romantic alliance is never cemented until he stops talking and succeeds in enticing her to dance with him. The duets themselves express completely the shifting moods of their ten-film love affair—the exhilaration of finding that their bodies speak the same choreographic language in "Isn't This a Lovely Day (To Be Caught in the Rain)?"; the affectionate bickering of "I'll Be Hard to Handle"; Astaire's sensuous seduction of the reluctant Rogers with "Night and Day."

Astaire even transforms the boy-loses-girl cliché imbedded in every movie musical plot into something honestly moving, simply by choreographing it to music. In *Swing Time,* Astaire sings the chilling threat that he's "Never Gonna Dance" again if Ginger walks out of his life, after which they re-enact in dance their entire courtship to that point, hauntingly capturing their shared knowledge of mutual loss. As they glide up opposite ends of the curved night-club stairway toward their separate futures, Fred

With Ginger Rogers in FOLLOW THE FLEET (1936)

and Ginger prove that in films at least, actions can indeed be more potent than words.

"Every once in a while I suddenly find myself dancing," Fred informs Ginger when his tapping interrupts her slumbers in the room below, early on in *Top Hat*. "It must be some sort of affliction," she retorts; fortunately incurable, it seems, as Astaire continued to find himself dancing until the demise of the big-studio musical in the mid-fifties. Dancing was never just the cleverest gimmick in Astaire's bottomless bag of cinematic tricks—it was as organic to his screen persona as walking or delivering lines. Astaire the performer was irresistibly compelled to express in dance whatever emotion was felt by Astaire the movie character. Even when his feet were rooted firmly to the sound-stage floor, every gesture or vocal inflection was orchestrated to some internal dance rhythm only he could hear.

Practically no other actor expends so much physical energy just to deliver dialogue as Astaire does—swiveling forward from the waist and leading with that over-abundant chin, Astaire continually pokes holes in the air around him for emphasis, strokes his jaw reflectively at his co-star's response, and shoves his hand into a convenient pants pocket to keep it still until the verbal exchange of the moment has run its course. Every motion Astaire makes on screen, however prosaic, seems just a beat away from becoming a dance cue, whether it's a stroll down a flight of stairs in *Funny Face* or a simple roll of dice in *Swing Time*. This is what makes the usually difficult transition from story into song look so spontaneous in Astaire's musicals. At some point the kinetic energy barely suppressed behind every Astaire gesture can no longer be contained—it has to be vented in an outburst of dance.

Astaire's prodigious footwork first attracted audiences to him in the thirties, but it was the new kind of screen hero that his dancing symbolized which really made him a star. The real world may have been torn asunder by mass unemployment, social unrest, and incipient fascism in the mid-thirties, but you'd never have known it from the likes of *Top Hat*. Even Busby Berkeley's opulent and absurd *Gold Diggers* series was populated with "forgotten men" and avaricious chorines suddenly down on their luck, but Astaire never had to grapple with such weighty economic problems. Although the Astaire/Rogers films were nominally set in locales whimsically referred to as "London," "Paris," and "New York," they really took place in the same interior decorator's *moderne* vision of Paradise. *Carefree* was the title given to Fred and Ginger's penultimate thirties romp, but it could have been applied just as easily to almost all of their team efforts.

From *Gay Divorcee* through *Shall We Dance* and the rest, Fred was eternally cast as the unflappable optimist confident that nothing important lies beyond his ample grasp. Despite his worldly manner and elegant attire, the Astaire persona is basically as innocent as Shirley Temple's. The on-screen Fred is motivated entirely by caprice, trusting everything to his own charm and the happy conjunction of fate. In a world in which the greatest obstacle to his happiness is one recalcitrant blonde, Astaire remains sunnily unreflective because such defenses are totally unnecessary. What audiences relished most about Astaire was not so much his effortless savoir-faire, but rather his savoir-vivre—the joyous gusto which permeates every appearance Astaire made on film.

This brand of naive vitality was not in itself a new quality in screen heroes; such earlier film stars as Douglas Fairbanks and Richard Dix had possessed it in abundance. But Astaire added a novel touch of sophistication to the mold, proving that such naughty screen continentals as Adolphe Menjou and Maurice Chevalier didn't hold the exclusive patent on urbanity and poise. Astaire fulfilled the American fantasy of an aristocracy based on charm and ability rather than in-

With Eleanor Powell in
*BROADWAY MELODY
OF 1940* (1940)

breeding. Moviegoers of the time could identify with Astaire's upper-class élan and elegance because he cannily infused it with a vigorous dose of home-grown raffishness. In whatever gilded watering spot he found himself, Astaire was very much the unpretentious American abroad—deflating European pomposity, scorning artiness in favor of swing and blues, reveling in his own slangy wisecracks. Sometimes the balance was shifted a bit too forcibly to bolster Astaire's link with the masses; Astaire practically induces lockjaw as the gum-chewing gob from *Follow The Fleet* without fooling anyone for a minute. Usually, however, Astaire realized that such sops to the hoi polloi weren't necessary, and reverted to his customary finesse the next time around.

Yet for all his elegant assurance, Astaire onscreen is anything but invulnerable. From his youthful escapades at RKO onward, Astaire has one perennial Achilles heel —his inveterate romanticism. At the start of most of his early vehicles, Astaire usually has immersed himself in the lackadaisical pursuit of pleasure; he's beguiling, but also a bit callow and purposeless. Love, always both instantaneous and eternal, gives his energies a focus and direction, as well as revealing his gay-young-blade bit for the rather shallow self-delusion it is. It's been widely noted that the secret behind the Astaire-Rogers chemistry was that she gave him an aura of sexuality he otherwise lacked, but Ginger's real accomplishment is that she forces him to grow up. There's usually a faint air of the overage fraternity pledge about Fred before genuine emotion takes over and carries him to adulthood. His friendly rival for the screen's dancing crown, Gene Kelly, often seems most comfortable roistering with the other boys like Donald O'Connor or Frank Sinatra, or else grappling choreographically with his own psyche. Astaire however, is never really complete psychologically until he has been mated with the appropriate female in dance.

Of course, the benefits of romance are mutual in Astaire's musicals. Just as he gains solidity from Ginger and her successors, Astaire grants them an outlet for their hidden sensuality. Most of Astaire's heroines possess a rather forbidding streak of prudery on first acquaintance; masked by an air of brisk practicality, they're really afraid of what they'll discover in themselves should they succumb to an Astaire seduction. Inevitably, Astaire's persistence always pays off—under his spell they reveal unexpected levels of feeling to themselves and the audience, and the result is exhilarating.

It's ironic that one of the most liberatingly erotic spirits in Ameri-

With Rita Hayworth in YOU WERE NEVER LOVELIER (1942)

can movies should have been encased in such an unprepossessing
form as Astaire's. Despite that ingratiatingly crinkly smile, Astaire
would hardly seem the stuff that
erotic dreams were made of. His
hollow-chested frame looks oddly
frail for a dancer, and apart from
his trademarked, snugly tailored
evening dress, clothes just hang
limply from his narrow shoulders.
Astaire's head looms hugely out of

proportion to his narrow torso, and
his features are really a cartoon-
ist's inspiration—the bulbous
domed forehead, those slightly pro-
truding poached eyes, and a craggy
nose veering downward towards his
jutting, peninsular jaw.

Even on the stage, where conventional good looks aren't essential
for romantic roles, Astaire's unusual physiognomy had proved
something of a handicap; usually he

found himself cast as sister Adele Astaire's platonic playmate while she blithely romanced some strapping young juvenile. Remarkably, Astaire turned this apparent liability into an asset once he exchanged Adele and the stage for Ginger et al. and the movies. For one thing, the erotic tension he created with his dancing partners came as an unexpected and delightful fringe benefit from a performer who otherwise seemed so asexual onscreen. For another, Astaire was so much the urbane charmer that handsomeness of the usual sort would really have been redundant. In fact, his looks gave Astaire a touch of fallibility his film personality desperately needed. Audiences might have resented his air of impeccable finesse if Astaire had possessed enormous physical magnetism to boot.

As it happened, the emotional chemistry that simmered between Astaire and Rogers proved so overpowering that it gravely threatened his screen future once their partnership came to its inevitable end. Obviously Ginger was fetching enough to be romanced convincingly by any of a host of regulation leading men, but many believed that Rogers alone held the elusive clue to Astaire's latent virility as a figure of romantic movie fantasy. This wasn't the only dilemma confronting Astaire as the forties succeeded the thirties, bringing with

them a whole new set of values and priorities. Black dinner jackets were exchanged for navy blues, and the airy sophistication that Astaire symbolized began to seem irrevocably anachronistic.

That likable proletarian Bing Crosby had been a popular movie crooner in the thirties while Astaire dominated the musical field; in the more homespun forties, their positions reversed, and twice Astaire found himself billed under Crosby while playing slightly effete capons whose restless feet posed no threat to Bing's vocalizing when it came to romance or show biz. During this uncertain period in Astaire's career, he seemed destined to travel an endless odyssey from studio to studio and ingénue to ingénue in search of the old magic and a new, more modish identity. No one was more conscious of this dilemma than Astaire himself; determined to relinquish the spotlight before public indifference forced him to do so, he opted for retirement in 1946. Ironically, it took Gene Kelly's broken ankle two years later to bring Astaire back.

The Astaire that emerged in the late forties at first glance seemed identical to the old one, but the passage of time and musical custom had brought some subtle changes. Astaire was fortunate enough to spend most of this period at MGM, where an accomplished team of directors, writers, choreographers, and technicians forged a new and exciting renaissance of the movie musical under the guardianship of producer Arthur Freed. This new era owed a good deal to the Astaire legacy of the thirties, but was guided by much more grandiose ambitions. Astaire's films of the previous decade had been intended as unpretentious, almost interchangeable diversions, whose slender strands of plot only served as groundwork for the musical interludes. The Freed unit at Metro conceived each effort as more of a distinctive event, combining conscious innovation with enormous technical expertise. The stories they contained, however frivolous, carried nearly equal weight as the songs and dances, and both elements were more closely interwoven; no longer was the hoofer-meets-loses-and-wins / decides-to-mount-show-with-pert-chorine considered sufficiently weighty a premise to sustain a musical.

Moreover, Astaire in the forties loomed less obviously as the *auteur* of the films he appeared in than had previously been the case. Such earlier Astaire directors as Mark Sandrich and George Stevens merely allowed Astaire to devise his own routines and photographed them as unobtrusively as possible. In contrast, directors like Vincente Minnelli, Stanley Donen, and Charles Walters had had extensive experience with musicals in both the theater and the movies, and accordingly exercised their right to shape the material with their own imprint as well. Lost was the sense of impromptu spontaneity that had been one of the most delightful qualities of Astaire's earlier work. Nor could clever scenarios, lively pacing, and technicolored visual dazzle quite compensate for the fact that the demise of composers like Kern and Gershwin and the relative decline of Porter and Berlin had left a vacuum that wasn't being filled by any of their successors. Yet at their considerable best, films like *The Band Wagon* and *Funny Face* combined the old effervescence with a new and exciting blend of opulence and inventiveness.

Astaire adapted most gracefully to the new regime. The later Astaire was more likely to be found in sport clothes than white tie and tails, his hyperkinetic boyishness easing into a kind of avuncular geniality. Middle age failed to dim the quick precision of his footwork, but it did tend to dilute his once-irrepressible amorousness on screen. Never really comfortable with the role of the casual womanizer, Astaire now usually played the pursued rather than the pursuer, generally in the guise of a myopic professional so immersed in his métier of the moment that two-thirds of the film elapsed before he could acknowledge the mutual attraction between himself and his co-star.

Complicating matters was the curious fact that although Astaire was allowed to age gradually but distinctly as his career evolved, his feminine counterparts remained perpetually twenty-five. This was hardly noticeable when Astaire frolicked with the decade-younger Ginger Rogers, but the chronological gap widened to twenty years with the likes of Garland and Charisse, and even thirty by the time he partnered such gamines as Audrey Hepburn and Leslie Caron. Astaire diluted the slight perversity of this by playing these roles as surrogate fathers turned reluctant lovers, but at any rate only the most literal-minded viewers really objected to these April-December casting ploys once the dialogue dissolved into the inevitable cue for an Astaire song and dance.

As Astaire neared the twentieth anniversary of his debut in pictures, he found himself in the odd position of being a certifiable screen legend who still participated as vigorously as ever in the field. His response was to become his own movie biographer; increasingly, his vehicles were not just tailored around his talents, but retold his past history as well. Critics and audiences had long since mentally cast Astaire as top-hatted Pygmalion to Ginger Rogers' satin-gowned Galatea; in *The Barkleys of Broadway* they re-enacted precisely that process, down to Rogers' rebellious urge to hang up her dancing pumps and go legit. The dogged quest for perfection in his work behind the scenes emerged full-blown on screen as a dour Astaire trained Judy Garland for the big time in *Easter Parade*. *Royal Wedding* glossily evokes the years of on- and offstage partnership with sister Adele; *The Band Wagon* purports to relate the theatrical comeback of one Tony Hunter, middle-aged movie hoofer *extraordinaire*, whose past hits included an epic entitled *Swinging Down to Panama*. Moreover, both *Funny Face* and *The Band Wagon* are loose pastiches of two of Astaire's greatest pre-Hollywood triumphs.

Astaire had endlessly proclaimed his refusal to find himself one day pirouetting across the screen arrayed with top hat, white hair, and crutches. Yet it was not Astaire's own decrepitude that prevented him from fulfilling this vision, but the death of the genre itself of which he was master. The disintegration of the big studios, the encroachment of television, and the advent of Elvis Presley and his ilk conspired to doom the large-scale movie musical to the purgatory of TV reruns and chink-in-the-wall revival houses. Astaire's usual outward composure was barely ruffled by this calamitous turn of events. Just as he had conquered radio in the thirties, he calmly shifted his efforts to the television studio, and his brilliant series of hour-long specials with new partner Barrie Chase bore him a number of Emmy awards and added new millions to the legions of admirers he already had.

Nor did the demise of the musical sound the death knell for Astaire's quarter-century-long film career; since 1959 he has from time to time returned to the screen to demonstrate that he had more to offer audiences than just a gracefully executed buck-and-wing. The nondancing Astaire affected a considerable range of screen guises, from the rueful intellectual of *On the Beach* to the gadabout socialite in *The Pleasure of His Company,* among others. By the sixties it seemed improbable that anyone as suave as Astaire could actually be just another Yank; the culture that had spawned his type seemed extinct, at least on this side of the Atlantic. Thus Astaire came to alternate playing dapper Englishmen and ingratiatingly corrupt smoothies, sometimes even incorporating the two. Many expressed surprise at Astaire's dramatic aptitude, but it had really always been there, overshadowed like his superb way with a song by his incomparable dancing.

When the sixties spawned a new cycle of musicals in the form of bloated superspectaculars based on

With Cyd Charisse in
SILK STOCKINGS (1957)

outmoded stage properties, logic dictated that at least one of them would call for a revival of his still formidable musical talents. The subsequent years have brought unabated activity to the now septuagenarian Astaire. Occasional movie character parts have been augmented by a steady parade of dramatic guest appearances on television. 1974 found the latter-day Astaire equally confronting his scintillating past in MGM's epitaph to itself, *That's Entertainment!*, as well as providing a rare human note amidst the cardboard chaos of *The Towering Inferno*. After a seventy-year career in show business, Astaire seems to defy human mortality with the same carefree ease with which his feet have always thwarted the pull of gravity. From exuberant juvenile to affable codger, Astaire's appeal has been timeless, but more than that, his legacy of musical achievements remains ageless.

FRED AND ADELE

For such a mundane center of midwestern commerce, Omaha, Nebraska, has spawned a remarkable number of prominent film performers, including Henry Fonda, Dorothy McGuire, Marlon Brando—and Fred Astaire. Born Fred Austerlitz in that city on May 10, 1899, Astaire derived his angular looks and distinctly non-Nebraskan manner from his father, a Viennese émigré who had deserted a lowly niche in the Austrian army for a more prosaic career in an Omaha brewery. From his mother, a beautiful and well-bred native Nebraskan, Astaire learned professional persistence and the importance of close family ties. And to his slightly older sister Adele he owed the fact that he ever embarked on a show business career at all.

The notion that second-born children are often overshadowed by their older siblings was clearly borne out in fact by Astaire's early life. From even before his birth until after he entered his thirties, both onstage and off, the premiere Astaire was elder sister Adele, while Fred contented himself with the eternal role of her likable kid consort. By all accounts, in infancy Fred was a completely ordinary, unremarkable child, but by the age of six Adele had already captivated her parents and the tutors at the local dancing academy with her high-stepping precocity. Her gifts persuaded the Austerlitzes to shoot for a career in vaudeville for their children, undeterred by the fact that little Fred as of yet showed neither interest nor aptitude for the dance. It was simply easier to bring Fred along while Mrs. Austerlitz mapped out Adele's assault on the big time.

Perky kid acts were an established staple in turn-of-the-century vaudeville, and Fred and Adele made unusually swift professional strides after their arrival in New York in 1904. While enrolled in the Claude Alvienne dancing school, Fred played Roxane to Adele's Cyrano de Bergerac, and with Alvienne they devised a wedding cake routine featuring Fred and Adele as toy newlyweds, followed by a devastating finish in which Adele impersonated a glass of champagne and Fred a boiled lobster. At least the act was novel, and it netted them engagements throughout New Jersey and Pennsylvania. This led to a booking on the prestigious Orpheum circuit, and for a couple of seasons they traversed the continent with their ingratiating antics.

Before long, however, it became obvious that not only were the

Adele at age ten,
Fred at age eight

Astaire tots outgrowing the act, but Adele had far outstripped her brother both in size and professional expertise. With their bookings dwindling rapidly, they settled with their mother in suburban New Jersey in the hopes that a two-year hiatus would give gangling Fred a chance to catch up with his accomplished sister. Soon thereafter they emerged with a new, more mature act concocted by famed theatrical coach Ned Wayburn. Their new song-and-dance specialty, "A Rainy Saturday," brought the now-adolescent Astaires a flurry of engagements but they were all strictly small-time; Adele's dainty aptitude

couldn't entirely camouflage her brother's ungainly poise and negligible stage presence. After a humiliating tour through a succession of midwestern fleapits, the Astaires were classed as a once-talented juvenile team whose appeal had faded along with their childhood.

In desperation they turned to another ex-vaudevillian turned coach for a solution, and it turned out to be the most auspicious step in their career. After long months spent mastering new adult routines and heeding the sage guidance of new teacher Aurelia Coccia, Fred and Adele painstakingly evolved into seasoned pros; Astaire later termed Coccia the strongest single influence on his later dancing style. Despite lowly billing and rowdy audiences, Fred and Adele gradually worked their way back to the coveted Orpheum circuit. While playing the Palace (in Chicago, that is—to their chagrin the Astaires never graced the boards of that venerated New York institution), they scored their first genuine triumph in vaudeville, after eleven years of effort. Although Adele's effervescence still overshadowed her brother's more earthbound personality, Fred increasingly took responsibility for the air of up-to-date sophistication that marked their act. Already Astaire had developed a remarkable instinct for spotting surefire songs and sketches; by 1916 he was interpolating melodies by the newly established Jerome Kern and the still-obscure Cole Porter into their routines.

In 1918 Fred and Adele forsook vaudeville forever when the Shubert brothers offered them a featured spot in the Broadway revue *Over the Top*. Another of the Shuberts' cut-rate carbons of Ziegfeld, the revue gambled on the premise that a line of lissome chorines would distract the public from the tatty backdrops and cobwebbed songs and comedy left over for the principals. The Astaires were further handicapped by the show's relentless emphasis on the charms of the decorative but limited Justine Johnstone, an ex-Glorified Girl predictably lifted by the Shuberts from the Ziegfeld ranks. Still, Fred and Adele had three numbers of their own (including, appropriately, the "Justine Johnstone Rag") and they attracted a bit of favorable notice from the reviewers, although one scribe loftily complained that they "smacked loudly of vaudeville."

During the following summer, the Shuberts re-engaged the Astaires for the somewhat more ambitious *Passing Show of 1918,* and this time their impact was undeniable. Although the show featured such stellar comedians as Willie and Eugene Howard, Frank Fay, and relative tyro Charles Ruggles, the critics reserved their most rhapsodic adjectives for the

Adele and Fred Astaire in 1915

Astaires. Unusually, Fred garnered the larger share of the team's praise, particularly for his farcical impersonation of a waiter at Childs Restaurant.

The Astaires next shifted their hijinks from revue to operetta, appearing the following year in Fritz Kreisler's melodic *Apple Blossoms*. Produced by Ziegfeld's closest rival, Charles Dillingham, the principal attraction in this lace valentine was stentorian-voiced matinée idol John Charles Thomas, while Fred and Adele provided doubtless welcome comic relief from all those high C's in waltz time. The show proved an enormous success and the Astaires' most prestigious showcase up to that point. Dillingham tried to

25

The Astaires in THE PASSING SHOW OF 1918

repeat the Thomas/Astaire formula in 1921 with *The Love Letter,* but the ingredients failed to coalesce a second time and the show quickly folded. The most notable thing about *The Love Letter* was that it introduced Fred and Adele's most renowned dance routine, the so-called "Oompah Trot." This sure-fire number was really amazingly simple: Adele would circle the stage like a marathon bicycle racer, Fred joined her for a few neck-and-neck laps, and the piece climaxed with a speedy, unexpected exit. The Astaires reprised this sequence innumerable times in a variety of shows for the rest of the decade, and Fred revived it amusingly with Gracie Allen for the funhouse sequence of *A Damsel in Distress* in 1937.

The Astaires didn't have long to brood about the failure of *The Love Letter,* for immediately thereafter they found themselves frolicking in a pleasant triviality called *For Goodness Sake,* at the lucrative salary of $800 a week. Their fleet-footed clowning to such whimsical numbers as "The Whichness of the Whatness" and "Oh Gee, Oh Gosh, Oh Golly," upstaged the flimsy matrimonial farce-plot to which they were but incidental, and almost single-handedly they guaranteed the show's moderate run. At the time, the critic for the New York *Post* typically wrote, "Adele is a most deliciously funny person, and Fred is not so very far behind her in ability."

Next came *The Bunch and Judy,* which offered the Astaires a Jerome Kern score and the first script expressly structured around their particular talents. The complicated libretto prophetically cast Adele as a musical-comedy star tempted by marriage to a Scottish aristocrat, while Fred was saddled with the already mildewed role of a comic thrust into the operetta lead after the star obligingly breaks his leg. The Astaires practically fractured theirs trying to put this material over, but the tepid reviews destined *The Bunch and Judy* to a rapid demise.

With their spirits dimmed by the fast failure of *The Bunch and Judy,* the Astaires eagerly grabbed an offer to transplant their previous show *For Goodness Sake* to England under the new title of *Stop Flirting!.* Fashionable London was bowled over by the breathless vitality of these madcap Americans, deeming them the most welcome import from the Colonies since that shocking young thespian, Tallulah Bankhead. *Stop Flirting!* ran well over a year in the West End, in contrast to the rather mild enthusiasm it had elicited in America. This reception made confirmed Anglophiles out of the Astaires—while Fred satiated his lifelong enthusiasm for horse racing at the track. Adele threaded her way through an

Adele and Fred in FOR GOODNESS SAKE (1922)

LADY BE GOOD (1924). With Kathlene Martyn and Adele Astaire

ardent throng of titled admirers.

To London's collective despair, in 1924 the Astaires returned to Broadway with the riotously successful *Lady Be Good,* which sported a Gershwin score, including "The Half-of-It-Dearie Blues," the wildly syncopated "Fascinating Rhythm," and the lilting title tune, plus the definitive Fred-and-Adele story line. Mirroring their private relationship, Adele enacted the impish gamine kept slightly in check by her lithe-limbed but more subdued sibling. Contemporary photographs of Astaire resemble a John Held Jr cartoon of the terribly up-to-date collegian vividly brought to life. Wearing a fashionably nonchalant air of jaded innocence, Astaire must have cut an immensely appealing figure on stage as Adele's dancing consort. But as usual, it was Adele who captivated everyone, including *The New York Times* which mildly remarked in its review, "Fred Astaire, too, gives a good account of himself." The Sunday *Times* piece was somewhat more balanced, claiming that "Just as (Gilbert and) Sullivan wrote the comedy of music, this art of the

Astaires is the comedy of the dance," but the die was cast nonetheless.

It all seemed so effortless for Adele. Even after each of their shows had settled into their runs, Fred spent countless hours polishing his routines. Yet like her fictional counterpart in *Royal Wedding*, Adele loathed wasting time rehearsing; considering her brother's rigors and incessant worrying droll and unnecessary, she dubbed him "Moaning Minnie," while blithely mesmerizing audiences without resorting to his monastic dedication.

After another extended London sojourn with the British edition of *Lady Be Good*, in 1927 Fred and Adele exhilarated Broadway once more with *Funny Face*, another collaboration with the Gershwins. This time Fred played wry guardian to three free-wheeling heiresses, the principal one being Adele, while foiling a bumbling safecracker (Victor Moore) who has designs on the family fortune. *Funny Face*, originally titled *Smarty*, was burdened with a nonsensical libretto, but a prodigally rich score, including "'S Wonderful," "He Loves and She Loves," and the title song, plus Fred's solo tap with chorus to "High Hat," while their familiar jog adapted to "The Babbitt and the Bromide" turned the musical into the usual Astaire romp. Their latest triumph intrigued Hollywood, still reeling from the impact of Jolson in *The Jazz Singer*, and before embarking on the usual London run of their latest hit, in 1928 the Astaires filmed a segment of *Funny Face* for Paramount's consideration. The test proved catastrophic, and the Astaires resolved to confine their hoofing to the stage, at least for the time being.

Unfortunately, their next stage effort was no more successful. Besides the Astaires, the 1930 *Smiles* sported Broadway's favorite dancing ingénue Marilyn Miller, a Vincent Youmans score, and the typically prodigal Ziegfeld production values, including an outsized array of the usual Glorified Girls. Yet all these elements were wasted on a leaden libretto concerning the unlikely alliance between a Salvation Army soul saver (Miller) and a high-living socialite (Astaire), while Adele and Eddie Foy, Jr., furnished the comic subplot. Both audiences and critics frowned sternly on *Smiles*, and it lasted a mere two months on Broadway.

Although the show proved a sorry disappointment, Fred and Adele offstage occupied themselves with events that would profoundly shape the course of their separate futures. As a favor to his old friend producer Alex Aarons, Fred agreed to restage a song which had proved troublesome during the tryouts of the new Gershwin musical, *Girl*

*FUNNY FACE (1927). With Betty Compton, Adele Astaire,
and Gertrude McDonald*

SMILES (1930). With Marilyn Miller

Crazy. The number was "Embraceable You" and the girl designated to sing it a red-haired ingénue named Ginger Rogers. The two became quite friendly and even spent a number of evenings together dancing in night clubs, but before long Ginger departed for California to pursue a movie career, and the two fell out of touch. Meanwhile Adele had renewed her acquaintanceship with a certain Lord Charles Cavendish, whom she had first met during the London run of *Funny Face.* Their romance blossomed and Adele finally announced that her next teaming with Fred would be her last before withdrawing permanently to Lismore Castle in Ireland as Lady Cavendish.

If Adele had to retire, *The Band Wagon* gave her the chance to exit with a gala flourish. At the time considered the *ne plus ultra* in wit and style, this revue glittered with the acerbic comedy of Howard Dietz's and George S. Kaufman's sketches, a blithe musical score by Dietz and Arthur Schwartz, a sumptuous production featuring Broadway's first-ever revolving stage, and the support of such droll people as Frank Morgan and Helen Broderick, who later added much merriment to Astaire's movie efforts. The plotless format allowed Astaire to display greater range than in any of his previous stage musicals. At one point he was decked out in tails for a light-hearted rendering of "New Sun in the Sky"; at another he was dressed down in tatters for the unexpectedly touching "Beggar Waltz," in which he dreams vainly of romancing haughty Viennese ballerina Tilly Losch. He and Adele amply vented their comic gifts as twin hoop-wielding brats wreaking mayhem on Paris, and in a sketch entitled "The Pride of the Claghornes," in which Southern gallant Fred refuses to wed local belle Adele when he learns she is still a virgin. *The Band Wagon* swirled to a climax as the revolving stage turned Bavarian merry-go-round and the entire cast lustily bellowed "I Love Louisa." True to her word, Adele sadly stepped off the carousel for good after the post-Broadway Chicago engagement of the show, wedding Cavendish in the summer of 1932.

As for Astaire, his first and only serious romance didn't take root until after he knew Adele was to forsake him and the stage for marriage and retirement. During the New York run of *The Band Wagon* he met a pretty, rather retiring member of Long Island's sporty set named Phyllis Potter, who knew little and cared less about the show business milieu in which Astaire thrived. To this point his immersion in his work had taken precedence completely over Astaire's private life, but Adele's departure and his growing attachment for Mrs. Potter reversed his priorities. They were married in July, 1933, just a few days before Astaire's auspicious first trip to Hollywood.

Despite this happy turn in his private affairs, after the close of *The Band Wagon* Astaire still faced the gravest professional crisis of his adult career. He had never set foot on stage before without his sister, and many doubted that he could sustain an entire musical on his own narrow shoulders. Nobody doubted his credentials as a dancer, but his brand of understated charm had never engendered the idolatry that surrounded the beloved Adele's. As a result Astaire knew that his next vehicle would be the most critical of his life; were it to fail, the blame would inevitably fall at his now-solo feet.

One solution was offered by producer Guthrie McClintic, Katharine Cornell's husband, who wanted Astaire for a straight dramatic role, but Astaire feared making such a drastic departure from his past work and opted instead for the genteel musical whimsies of *Gay Divorce*. Among the show's attributes were an attractive Cole Porter score and an alluring new partner for Astaire in Claire Luce,

THE BANDWAGON (1931).
With Tilly Losch

an ersatz night of adultery had long since lost its blush of titillation by 1932.

The first-night critics loathed *Gay Divorce* with near unanimity, but their reaction to an Adele-less Fred proved somewhat more equivocal. The show managed to run a respectable seven months, largely due to the immediate popularity of its principal song, "Night and Day" and the widespread circulation of cut-priced tickets. In truth, "Night and Day" not only salvaged *Gay Divorce* but also revealed a previously undiscovered facet of Astaire's performing talents. Astaire had never even remotely been considered a romantic figure on stage before this musical, and he still had trouble convincing audiences of his manly allure in the show's non-musical stretches. But once he and Luce undulated to the insistent rhythms of "Night and Day" the erotic tension was undeniable, giving Astaire a new dimension that would sustain his work for the next three decades.

Although nobody realized it at the time, Astaire's somewhat inconclusive solo debut marked his farewell to Broadway, thanks to new developments three thousand miles away in Hollywood. The overwhelming reaction to Warner Brothers' backstage musical *42nd Street* had revived the dormant genre of the movie musical overnight, as each of the studios fran-

who rather resembled Ginger Rogers on a slightly higher social plane. Unfortunately, its libretto seemed to have been culled from scraps out of Noel Coward's wastebasket; for all its airs of soigné sophistication, this tale of a writer's entanglement in a young lady's attempt to gain a divorce through

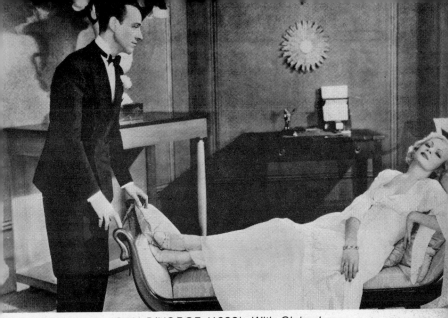

GAY DIVORCE (1932). With Claire Luce

tically outdid each other trying to top the original. RKO's entry in the song-and-dance sweepstakes was to be the large-scale *Flying Down to Rio*, and they reserved a prominent part in it for Astaire. The possibilities of this new medium greatly intrigued him; apart from everything else, the movies offered him the chance to forge an independent public identity for himself, freed from the specter of his sister, who was as unknown to the mass film audience as he was.

For these reasons Astaire jumped at the $1500-a-week contract that RKO dangled before him, and planned to begin his assault on the movies as soon as *Gay Divorce* finished its New York run. Nevertheless, he remained clear-headed enough not to close off all his other options; whatever the outcome of *Flying Down to Rio*, Astaire still had contracted to bring *Gay Divorce* to London upon completing his movie debut. Such precautions had a tinge of the old "Moaning Minnie" paranoia to them, but Astaire had every right to be apprehensive—for all their outpourings of encouragement, the executives at RKO really had no clear idea of what they were going to do with him once he met their challenge.

Astaire arrived in Hollywood during the summer of 1933, only to discover that the much-touted *Flying Down to Rio* had bogged down in a mire of pre-production problems. In the meantime RKO agreed to loan Astaire to David O. Selznick, who had recently left that studio for a thorny niche in his father-in-law L. B. Mayer's domain, MGM. Selznick's current project was a Clark Gable-Joan Crawford musical extravaganza called *Dancing Lady*, which RKO hoped would painlessly introduce Astaire to movie audiences, while MGM expected him to add a touch of prestige to the raffish proceedings. Yet Astaire's screen debut is so fleeting and carelessly conceived that his impact is at best subliminal.

Calculated to restore Crawford to popularity after a recent career setback, *Dancing Lady* focused its energies entirely on rehashing the usual Crawford ode to social mobility in the saucy "showbizzy" mode popularized the year before by *42nd Street*. *Dancing Lady* did a great deal for Crawford at the time, but absolutely nothing for anyone else involved in the enterprise. Gable loathed following so closely in Warner Baxter's footsteps as the hyperthyroid Broadway Svengali who brusquely shoves Joan to the top, and he finally had to be strong-armed into tackling the part.

As for Astaire, he is only on hand

A FINE ROMANCE

long enough to provide an escort at Joan's screen coronation as queen of terpsichore. Cast as himself, he is whisked on briefly halfway through the film for a very short tap with Crawford, then disappears until the gargantuan production number that climaxes the film. This sequence indicates why most of the MGM musicals of the thirties were so uninspired; like most of its later counterparts, it imitates Busby Berkeley's trademarked opulence and scope without capturing his witty perversity or keen eye for striking images. Fred and Joan begin with a song and dance in evening clothes to "Heigh Ho, The Gang's All Here" before gliding on a magic carpet to a German beer garden for a deadpan "Let's Go Bavarian" in lederhosen and dirndls. Clearly derived from *The Band Wagon*'s "I Love Louisa," it reaches for the same sly humor but the result is merely arch and uneasy. Perversely, the sequence manages to show off Crawford's inadequacies as a dancer while reducing him to dapper anonymity at the same time. The number is a cinch for Astaire but all that's really required of him is to smile a lot, get the steps right, and make sure Crawford doesn't fall off that flying carpet.

If RKO had worried about how to peg Astaire since his arrival in Hollywood, certainly his appearance in *Dancing Lady* didn't provide them with any useful hints. In 1933 most movie leading men were either tough like Cagney or handsome like Gary Cooper and Cary Grant, or both simultaneously, like Gable. If Astaire resembled any established film favorite it was Stan Laurel, so when *Flying Down to Rio* finally reached the cameras, the studio took the easy way out —they cast him as the leading man's cheery, asexual sidekick. By pure chance, old acquaintance Ginger Rogers was brought in to play his female counterpart, although she was certainly anything but sexless. Despite having played leads in a few minor efforts, Rogers hadn't made much progress during her three years in Hollywood. Still very much the soubrette, she was best known for a few tart bits in the Busby Berkeley musicals, especially for singing "We're in the Money" in pig Latin for *Gold Diggers of 1933*. As far as Ginger was concerned, *Flying Down to Rio* was just another assignment; no one suspected that one of the most delightful interludes in screen history was being inaugurated in that instant when Ginger pulled Fred onto the dance floor for a whack at the Carioca.

DANCING LADY (1933). Fred and Joan Crawford "go Bavarian."

DANCING LADY (1933). On the set with Joan Crawford, Clark Gable, chorus, and crew

FLYING DOWN TO RIO (1933). With Ginger Rogers and the chorines

Never were musicals more self-consciously escapist than during the depths of the Depression, and *Flying Down to Rio* takes the concept literally. The entire film centers around the notion of escape through the most glamorous means imaginable in 1933—the air. Extending the Good Neighbor Policy to ludicrous lengths, Yank bandleader Gene Raymond pursues reluctant Brazilian debutante Dolores Del Rio all the way from Miami to Rio de Janeiro by air. They fall in love in his private plane, indulge in lovers' tiffs while airborne, and are even married aloft by an obliging pilot as Raymond's Latin rival Raul Roulien dejectedly .parachutes to terra firma. Even the film's title song is performed by several dozen masochistic chorus girls frolicking precariously on airplane wings.

As their lowly billing below the title indicates, Fred and Ginger just hover around the sidelines, functioning mainly as a sort of wise-cracking Greek chorus to the amorous doings of Raymond and Del Rio in the foreground. As band singer Honey Hale and accordionist/best pal Fred Ayres, Rogers and Astaire are so peripheral to the plot that there isn't even a secondary love story built around them—they're just chums thrown together because they work for the

FLYING DOWN TO RIO (1933).
With Dolores Del Rio

Makes Me" in her saucy nasal style while arrayed in a transparent pre-Frederick's of Hollywood black gauze gown. Astaire tangos with Del Rio to "Orchids in the Moonlight" with negligible impact, but makes up for it with his whirlwind tap reprise of "Music Makes Me"—his first solo dance in movies and an exhilarating promise of what was to come.

In between, of course, Fred and Ginger join heads and hips for the Carioca, their first dance duet, to the amazement of the ersatz Brazilian throng, and in Ginger's words, "show them a thing or three." Actually, compared to their later teamwork, this routine is engaging enough but hardly galvanizing. They are hamstrung by the gimmicky choreography and are only allowed two brief run-throughs before alternate hordes of black and white extras in black-and-white costumes overrun the Latin-*moderne* café set. Yet already there is something special about their choreographed byplay on the dance floor—a delicious sense of conspiracy that passes between Fred and Ginger as they gaze at each other while dancing.

The only major musical sequence which doesn't focus on Fred and Ginger's accomplishments is the whoops-a-daisy "Flying Down to Rio" number itself, and even here Astaire gets to let loose with a chorus of the song as the chorines soar

same band. Yet although Fred is forced to exude nothing but boyish heartiness in near fatal doses, and Honey is just another Berkeley chorine with a few more lines, Astaire and Rogers positively shine with high spirits compared to the corny swill that surrounds them.

Raymond and Del Rio are as vacuous as they are beautiful, and while the heroine grappled in vain with lines like, "When a Brazilian girl starts something, she must finish it," Fred and Ginger cornered the sprightly Vincent Youmans score. Besides leading the airborne division in the title number, Ginger belts the infectious "Music by. "Sounds like a new thrill," mutters one hapless blonde as she is strapped in place on the wing of a biplane, and indeed it is. This is probably the only production number in all the Astaire-Rogers pictures that really matches Busby Berkeley for spectacular silliness, and it provides the film with a visual lift which Thornton Freeland's earthbound direction otherwise lacks.

The public's eagerness for an immediate Fred-and-Ginger reunion, in romantic close-up this time, wasn't lost on RKO for long. In its search for an immediate follow-up for the new team, the studio quite logically adapted Astaire's last stage vehicle for the screen. To the play's basic skeleton, RKO grafted some of *Flying Down to Rio's* more palatable elements—impossibly glamorous albino-white settings depicting faraway locales, and a few intimate songs and dances culminating in one garish extravaganza keyed to the strains of a novel dance routine. The result was *The Gay Divorcee* (1934), and for all its rough edges it immediately establishes the Astaire-Rogers team persona that would joyfully thrive with minor variations through the eight subsequent movies they were to make together.

The breezy juvenile Fred portrayed in *Flying Down to Rio* has grown into someone infinitely more engaging with *The Gay Divorcee*.

FLYING DOWN TO RIO (1933). Fred and Ginger do "the Carioca."

As classy professional dancer Guy Holden, Astaire has been transformed into a foot-loose, unpretentiously urbane youth who follows his blithe whims to whichever glittering locale they may lead. He protests that dancing is his vocation and nothing more, but this is just an idle pose—it grants him a delirious outlet for his high spirits and irrepressible longing for romance. He sees himself as a gallant lady-killer, but his corny verbal pitches really just expose his nervous gawkiness to the withering gaze of a sage surveyor of men like Ginger's Mimi Glossop. But naturally, when words are succeeded by music, he

THE GAY DIVORCEE (1934): Fred watches as Edward Everett Horton and Betty Grable dance.

THE GAY DIVORCEE (1934). With Ginger Rogers

THE GAY DIVORCEE (1934). With Edward Everett Horton

actually becomes the adroit and tender romancer he has always envisioned himself to be.

As Mimi, Ginger here makes the transition from the saucy starlet of yore into the swank leading lady of everything that followed. Her flowered frocks, cheeky pout, and elaborately curled coiffure are holdovers from her fast-fading starlet days, but she has already assumed that pose of all-knowing innocence which became her hallmark for the rest of the decade with Astaire. Now an unmistakable bourgeoise, on the surface Ginger has a dim view of everybody's motives, particularly those exhibited by men. Yet like Fred's self-delusions, Ginger's cynicism is really just a defense mechanism. Her

irritation with Fred's unquashable advances merely constitutes an inescapable ground rule for screen courtship in the thirties. Once she stops protesting long enough to be wooed by Fred and the music, emotion overwhelms her scruples and her reserve disintegrates; at heart she is just as romantic as he is, if a bit more wary. Together they generate such extraordinary electricity that even the film's most glaring flaws are rendered irrelevant.

It's odd that *The Gay Divorcee*'s plot so alienated the drama critics in New York, as here it seems ideally serviceable, though a little on the long-winded side. Like many of their later sagas, it's really a tale of love temporarily thwarted because Ginger has mistaken Fred

THE GAY DIVORCEE (1934).
"Night and Day"

gallery of middle-aged grotesques, both male and female. Recruited from the stage version are paid co-respondent Erik Rhodes, an irrepressible Italianate tenor who specializes in effete indignation and outlandish distortions of English, plus whimsical waiter Eric Blore, who spent the next few years in a perpetual snit over the misconduct of his social better Edward Everett Horton, cast as Astaire's incurably befuddled confidant. On the distaff side, Alice Brady plays the first in a succession of Ginger's gimlet-eyed duennas.

Much more time is spent with these supporting players than is entirely necessary, but luckily the balance is redressed in the musical numbers, which are both delightful in themselves and for what they reveal about Fred and his inamorata as the film unreels. Astaire wastes no time before showing off his gifts—less than five minutes after the fade-in, Fred is shoved onto the dance floor to tap for his supper, as he can't pay the check for his meal in a Parisian restaurant. Irritated at being imposed upon to dance while on holiday, he lets his body crumple with boredom, but soon the rhythm of "Don't Let It Bother You" invades him and he is off and gyrating frenziedly in spite of himself. Meeting Ginger finally gives him something important to dance about, and to the tune of "A Needle in a

for somebody else, until she finally acknowledges the affection she has felt for him from the beginning. In this case Ginger finds herself in London for a divorce from her elusive geologist husband, and she confuses Fred with the professional gigolo hired to pose as her lover so she can get her decree. Ultimately she realizes that not only has Astaire wooed her for purely personal reasons, but that her detested spouse is a bigamist, making the divorce unnecessary after all.

As comic embellishment Fred and Ginger are surrounded by a

laystack" the definitive Astaire ersonality really emerges for the irst time. No longer just breezily apping in a void, Astaire incorporates both the character's emoions and every object he touches nto the fabric of his dance. First inging with urgency of his need to ind Ginger again, Astaire then oars over his drawing-room sofa, ails around the room while tapping is heels in midair, and lands with ease upright on the seat of a conenient chair, having meanwhile changed from dressing gown to lapper street clothes without breaking his stride for an instant.

Halfway through the film, when Astaire (and the audience) have begun to wonder if he is ever going o make any headway with Ginger, e cajoles her into the rapturous "Night and Day," and their magical partnership suddenly takes light. Astaire sings the one Porter song retained from the play with incredible fervor and passion, and hen tops this intensity as he blocks Rogers' dogged attempt at retreat and literally pulls her into his choreographed thrall. "Night and Day" doesn't have the technical polish of most of their later dialogues in the guise of dance—the steps have a self-conscious edge and Ginger has a few unsteady moments that betray her inexperience at this sort of thing—but that kind of perfection would soon come with time and practice.

THE GAY DIVORCEE (1934).
Dancing with Ginger to
"the Continental"

The number's strong point is its heady emotionalism; some of their duets conveyed rapture, others poignance, but this one is all about undisguised physical longing. Between them Astaire and Rogers ignite such a potent aura of elegant sensuality that it seems almost indelicate to watch. As the number concludes, Rogers glances up at Astaire with a look of dazed, erotic wonder on her face—this ought to have been ludicrous, but no other reaction could have sufficed. No wonder Astaire opposed an excess

45

of smooching in his films with Rogers, for it would have been quite superfluous.

After "Night and Day," "The Continental" seems rather piffling, for all its gaudy grandeur. The number adheres closely to the recipe concocted by choreographer Dave Gould the year before for "The Carioca": take one catchy tune, wreak infinite rhythmic variations on it through an endless string of reprises, add a few solo singers and dancers for variety, overwhelm them with dozens of hyperglandular choristers in black and white costumes, place the whole thing on a gargantuan white set, and photograph it from the perspective of a passing seagull. When all this activity subsides sufficiently, Fred and Ginger burst on and display another facet to their dancing teamwork. Gliding around each other with arms tilted like nuzzling biplanes, they are not merely proficient; more important, they seem to be having a perfectly marvelous time. The infectious afterglow they create even makes tolerable the last music-less fifteen minutes devoted to tying up the loose strands of that insistent plot. *The Gay Divorcee* fulfilled the promise of Fred's accidental encounter with Ginger in *Flying Down to Rio* more fully than anyone had the right to expect.

Astaire and Rogers' overnight following had only three months to catch their breath before *Roberta,* (1935) treated them with a third teaming. For the only time in their joint career, Fred and Ginger shared the limelight and halved their screen footage with another RKO luminary, but they really got the better half of the deal; while Irene Dunne dispatches with the soggy plot, Fred and Ginger have all the fun. As in *Flying Down to Rio,* Fred and Ginger spend most of their time clucking their tongues over someone else's bumpy love affair. And like *The Gay Divorcee, Roberta* had been adapted from a successful Broadway musical whose libretto was decidedly the least of its virtues.

Of all the most prominent songsmiths of the thirties, Jerome Kern was undoubtedly the most anachronistic, and at heart *Roberta* is just a lavender-and-lace operetta gussied up in *moderne* crêpe de Chine. Dunne portrays an English-educated Russian princess whom fate and Lenin have reduced to designing clothes for the House of Roberta in Paris. But the revolution was nothing compared to her emotional trauma when she meets Randolph Scott, the hayseed American nephew of the proprietress. The puritanical Scott inherits the shop after Roberta's death, and their romance hits a snag when the jealous Irene sells a flashy black satin number to Scott's predatory American fiancée, infuriating the righteous hero. All too predictably, they are reunited at the couture-drenched finale, with a knowing assist from those caustic cupids, Fred and Ginger.

Periodically Fred and Ginger stroll through this morass, blithely immune to the musty kitsch that saturates the screen whenever they disappear from view. Having proved their viability as a team with *The Gay Divorcee*, here they simply bask in the effortless pleasure of each other's company. As band-leader Huck Haines (of the Wabash Indianians) Fred trots out his best boisterous-plebeian-abroad manner, immensely amused to learn that the Countess Scharwenka, singing sensation of Paris, is none other than one Lizzie Gatz, with whom he enjoyed many barnyard romps before she lost her consonants and acquired that title. With her guttural snarl and seething temperament, Ginger wittily mocks Lyda Roberti, billed as "Broadway's preferred Polish blonde" and Rogers' predecessor in the role. Usually Ginger stalks off airily at Fred's innocent transgressions, but here they are conspirators in the same joke.

Their lovelorn co-star Dunne, who doted on such things, dispatches with Kern's more soothing refrains. She flutters resplendently to "Lovely to Look At," while her sotto voce rendition of "Yesterdays" to the moribund Mme.

ROBERTA (1935).
"I'll Be Hard to Handle"

Roberta (Helen Westley) provides the film with one of its few really tender moments. Unfortunately she drowns the film's prettiest melody, "Smoke Gets in Your Eyes," in a sea of gallantry, suppressing her tears behind a steely grin for the sake of her entourage as Scott drunkenly walks out of her life. Meanwhile Fred and Ginger extend their playful camaraderie into the cheerier stuff Kern has reserved for them. Fred stomps out the sprightly "Let's Begin," and Ginger bellows a warning of her mercurial Polish nature with "I'll Be Hard to Handle." Wryly reversing their

47

usual pattern, Fred adamantly replies "I Won't Dance" to Ginger's entreaties, despite her flattering claim that "When you dance, you're charming and you're gentle/'Specially when you do the Continental." Of course, Astaire succumbs to the mood of the moment and placates her with an animated, loose-jointed tap. Although the Astaire-Rogers numbers have practically no relation to *Roberta*'s plot, they spring spontaneously from the emotional logic of the scene at hand. During "I'll Be Hard to Handle", Fred and Ginger casually complete the dia-logue with their feet, he circling her placatingly, she shaking her tresses and stamping on his toes, until they twirl speedily to a halt, helpless with mirth.

As usual they are implicated in the lush production number that culminates the film—this time a musical fashion show featuring Fred's combo, Irene and her massive white furs, and every other starlet on the RKO lot (including a platinum-blonde, feather-smothered Lucille Ball), arrayed in an assortment of remarkably hideous gowns. It's all rather empty and ostentatious until Fred and

ROBERTA (1935). Dancing with Ginger to
"Smoke Gets in Your Eyes"

TOP HAT (1935). With Ginger Rogers and Erik Rhodes

Ginger reprise "Smoke Gets in Your Eyes" and introduce an entirely unexpected note of pathos into their sham surroundings. Heads lowered, gliding side by side as close as possible without quite touching, they seem lost in a thought too poignant and intimate to share with anyone else. The tempo builds, the steps turn more complex, but the mood persists. This sequence completes Ginger's astonishing metamorphosis from cheeky coquette to supple enchantress; as for Astaire, it confirms what "Night and Day" had provocatively suggested. The breezy entertainer that was always Astaire

had learned to touch the heart as well. Appropriately, *Roberta* concludes not with the expected clinch between Irene Dunne and Randolph Scott, but rather on the effervescence of Fred and Ginger's blazing recap of "I Won't Dance."

If anyone still doubted that Astaire and Rogers in tandem had become RKO's principal adornment, the acclaim accorded *Roberta* dispelled all qualms. By 1935 the studio firmly committed its efforts to maintain its most lucrative asset, and had assembled a formidable team of specialists to insure the team's smooth transition from vehicle to vehicle. Among these were Pandro S. Berman, producer of all the Astaire-Rogers RKO efforts, Mark Sandrich, who directed five of them in his smooth, sympathetic manner, and Allan Scott, who co-wrote everything from *Roberta* through *Carefree* and thus was largely responsible for having shaped Astaire and Rogers into those beloved screen characters, Fred-and-Ginger. Perhaps most indispensable of all these movie artisans was choreographer Hermes Pan, who co-designed and rehearsed all Astaire's routines with the star and his pianist weeks before shooting commenced on each film.

After *Roberta*'s triumph, Berman, Sandrich et al. next applied themselves to what turned out to be the quintessential film of the entire Astaire-Rogers series. There is no particular reason why *Top Hat* (1935) should have been the supremely diverting achievement it is. Irving Berlin's first score for Astaire is unfailingly melodic, but not measurably superior to his contributions to *Follow the Fleet* later on, not to mention Gershwin's songs for *Shall We Dance* or Kern's in *Swing Time*. Although the Allan Scott-Dwight Taylor screenplay was the first conceived from scratch for Astaire, there's hardly an original idea in it; the plot, tone, characterizations and even most of the locales are lifted bodily from Taylor's *The Gay Divorcee*. And

certainly Mark Sandrich's helming holds no revelations after his work on the same film.

What made *Top Hat* so special was that it occurred at a singular crossroads in Astaire's professional relationship with Rogers. After three momentum-building teamings, their miraculous chemistry had yet to lose its freshness, while their teamwork had achieved an ease and precision that only time and familiarity can give. *Top Hat* radiates with self-confidence; all concerned know exactly what they're doing and how to do it, and revel in every audacious move they make.

Like every really memorable movie, *Top Hat* takes place in its own freshly minted world, one that resembles a precocious child's wistful daydream of sophisticated adulthood. In this naïve fantasy, blithe adults do intoxicatingly grown-up things like disporting in night clubs disguised as Italian maritime cities, dressing up in staggeringly chic raiments, and trading caustic witticisms with gleeful panache. So inured are they to this gilded life that none of its pleasures seem to surprise them; Fred for one isn't fazed at all by the fact that his London boudoir resembles a larger, albino version of the Gentlemen's Lounge at Radio City Music Hall.

Yet for all their urbanity, Fred and his cohorts glide through *Top*

TOP HAT (1935). The "Top Hat" number

TOP HAT (1935). Fred and Ginger, dancing "Cheek to Cheek"

Hat with the guileless gusto of eternal Peter Pans. Villainy, cruelty, or even genuine cynicism are nowhere to be seen, and even sex and its complications have only the most minimal connection with the frivolous male/female skirmishes which spark the film. Rogers owes her satiny surroundings to her métier as model and traveling companion to dress designer Erik Rhodes, but for all his ardor, there isn't even a hint of impropriety to this arrangement—and not only because of Ginger's traditional wariness toward the opposite sex. She waxes indignant when she thinks the flirtatious Astaire is actually Helen Broderick's philandering husband—not that she is shocked by the sordid prospect of sexual infidelity; rather Fred has simply broken the rules of convention that a nice girl like Ginger holds dear.

As for Fred, his longing for Ginger is boyish and tender, but hardly tainted by actual lust, an instinct that in any case was rarely part of his acting repertoire. And if Fred and Ginger are youthfully innocent, their assorted friends and nemeses seem positively infantile. Erik Rhodes' couturier is the Neapolitan joker in the deck, whose incessant outbursts seem to have been transcribed by Gertrude Stein during a bumpy stopover in Capri. Scowling butler Eric Blore and twittering employer Edward Everett Horton bicker like preschoolers over a half-eaten lollipop. Only owlish, sardonic Helen Broderick, Horton's nominal spouse, seems to have a frame of reference broader than the petty spheres of her male counterparts, and a brain large enough to cope with what she sees.

Although the antics of these zanies take too much precious time away from Astaire and Rogers, *Top Hat*'s simple saga of mistaken identity provides the most adroitly fashioned showcase for their gifts they were ever to find together. Their initial meeting is the cleverest of the entire series. In a sequence reminiscent of *Gay Divorcee*'s "A Needle in a Haystack," Astaire sings an anthem of independence from emotional entanglements to the tune of "No Strings"; ironically his exhilarating romp through his London digs awakens his future heartthrob on the floor below. Ginger vents her infinite spleen, as usual, and he placates her enchantingly by soothing her to sleep with the suavest of sand-muffled softshoes on the floor above her boudoir.

Ginger discovers their affinity is mutual when, after a canter through a London park, they take refuge in a covered bandstand from a sudden squall, and he sings of the fortuitousness of it all in the ingratiating "Isn't This a Lovely Day (To Be Caught in the Rain)?"

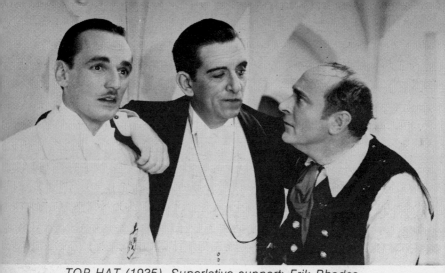

TOP HAT (1935). Superlative support: Erik Rhodes, Edward Everett Horton, and Eric Blore

This is perhaps the most breathtakingly charming of all their duets. It begins simply, with Astaire unlimbering a bit and Ginger saucily mimicking his steps. Ginger's aptitude naturally clinches his regard for her, and their rapport soars in that exhilarating moment when a clap of thunder resounds, the tempo accelerates, and they whirl as one at blinding speed around the gazebo. At the end they shake hands in jaunty acknowledgment of what has just happened—but the audience doesn't need such signals. Without a word or even a kiss, Fred and Ginger have discovered a magical kinship that couldn't be imagined with any other partner.

Some reels later, Astaire tries to assuage Ginger's latest fit of indignation with "Cheek to Cheek," in which he informs her that he would rather dance with her than do any other earthly thing. Their stately teamwork here is glorious to watch, though more studied and less erotic than "Night and Day" and "Smoke Gets in Your Eyes." The immutably somber expression on their faces are their greatest achievement under the circumstances. Ginger's feathered gown provoked many technical hassles and considerable mirth at the time, as it proceeded to molt profusely under the glare of the studio lights. Fred dubbed Ginger "Feathers" in tribute, and mockingly re-created the incident with Judy Garland in *Easter Parade* a decade later.

"The Piccolino" fulfills the requirement for the usual extravaganza, and as ever Fred and Ginger join forces for an exuberant spree of tandem twirling and heel kicking, whenever they can elbow their way through all those indefatigable chorus kids clambering over the white-lacquered Venetian monstrosity of a set. The subsequent finale precisely follows the *Gay Divorcee* pattern, but like everything else about *Top Hat,* with an added soupcon of polish and élan. Instead of doing the obvious and merely walking arm and arm toward the seaplane that will carry them to matrimony, Astaire and Rogers tear into a brief reprise of "The Piccolino, whirling madly out of the camera frame for the final fade-out.

Its unbeatable mixture of energy and know-how made *Top Hat* the most popular of all nine entries in the Astaire-Rogers series. More significantly, the film rewarded audiences with the definitive portrait of the Astaire screen persona; so indelible was its impact that reverberations of it have haunted his work and his image ever since. *Top Hat* lifted Astaire from the novel to the irreplaceable. As professional dancer and free spirit Jerry Travers, Astaire made sophistication respectable by democratizing it with a touch of humanity. Jerry may travel in the most exalted circles, but pomposity or tradition never intimidate him. The first thing he does onscreen is to wreak havoc in a zombified men's club by drumming his feet like gunfire in gleeful farewell to all that stuffiness. Throughout *Top Hat,* Astaire exudes the expected airy finesse, but most important, he seems unaware that anything but luck and energy separate him from more plebeian mortals.

Everything in life is easy for Jerry Travers/Astaire, and his grace is so self-effacing that he makes everything he does look easy as well. As Jerry whirls with glee around his hotel room, Astaire makes dancing look like the most natural and effortless human activity imaginable, and his nonchalance even takes the starch out of the formal attire that was his trademark. Moviegoers had seen innumerable leading men encased like penguins in evening clothes, but only Astaire made them seem as comfortable as everyday worsted.

Kern, Porter, and Vincent Youmans had already provided Astaire with a host of marvelous melodies to perform, but it took Irving Berlin to create the song that summed up Astaire's singular effervescence. Like most of Berlin's best-known songs, "Top Hat" is essentially a very simple lyric linked with an uncomplicatedly catchy tune. Astaire takes this custom-made melody and choreographically fleshes it out into something unique and unmistakably his. Astaire begins the routine as a dazzling virtuoso tap, aided only by his gleaming walking stick and backed up by a row of in-

TOP HAT (1935). "The Piccolino"

nocuous chorus boys in identical natty dress. By the time the number has ended, Astaire has transformed the chorus into enemies and human targets both seen and unseen, and his cane has metamorphosed into a variety of wittily lethal weapons.

Astaire was famous for constantly shifting tempos and rhythm in his routines, for the sake of variety and momentum—here he shifts mood as well. The carefree entertainer, literally dancing rings around his cane, gives way to a cautious, solitary figure crouching in anticipation of some invisible, nocturnal terror; then the lights onstage find him changed into a wry marksman taking pot shots at a human shooting gallery, mowing down his quarry with a deafening volley of taps, and picking off the last survivor through the mimed twang of his cane turned bow-and-arrow. Astaire had first concocted this number for his 1930 stage musical *Smiles,* but *Top Hat* gave it immortality. Of all the diverse solo numbers he ever tackled on screen, this is the quintessential moment; eleven years later in *Blue Skies,* Astaire capped his intended swan song to the movies with the closest possible facsimile to this routine, again set to the upbeat mood of an Irving Berlin tune.

After the pinnacle of *Top Hat,* anything Astaire and Rogers attempted was destined to be a letdown. This proved to be the case with *Follow the Fleet* (1936), although the studio took great pains to avoid comparison with Astaire's previous triumph. Based on a stage comedy which had also engendered Vincent Youmans' *Hit the Deck, Follow the Fleet* replaced Astaire's top hat with a jaunty sailor cap, banished the usual stock company of supporting players, and transplanted him back to his native soil for the first time since the opening reels of *Flying Down to Rio.* As in *Roberta,* Fred and Ginger corner the market on rollicking good spirits while love's banal tribulations fall on the burly shoulders of Randolph Scott again, this time paired with mousy chanteuse Harriet Hilliard. Bolstered by another sheaf of melodic Berlin originals, Astaire and Rogers endow *Follow the Fleet* with their customary jubilance and expertise. Yet even their most electric display of musical pyrotechnics can't quite compensate for a script which doesn't suit Astaire's personality or mesh with the score as snugly as usual.

There is a certain pleasant novelty involved in shoving Fred and Ginger a few pegs lower on the social scale than before. Astaire sheds his consonants along with his classy attire to play seaman Bake Baker, ex-half of a cheesy vaudeville act ("Baker and Martin, High Class Patter and Genteel Dancing"), which broke up when part-

FOLLOW THE FLEET (1936). With Randolph Scott and a sea-going chorus

ner Ginger decided to go solo both onstage and off. Rogers, however, has discovered to her chagrin that "They're not interested in a girl dancing alone unless she had a fan," so she's reduced to entertaining the troops as featured attraction in a waterfront dance hall. (Among her dime-a-dance cronies are Betty Grable, demoted from her solo status in *The Gay Divorcee,* and wisecracking Lucille Ball, graduated from her silent walk-ons in *Roberta* and *Top Hat.*)

The trouble starts for performers and audiences alike when they are upstaged by an insipid romance between fickle Scott and steadfast Hilliard, cast as Rogers' demure schoolteacher sister. Their tearful spats and wan reunions are reminis-

cent of the less bearable stretches of *Roberta,* made drearier still since, both vocally and histrionically, Hilliard is no Irene Dunne. Moreover, this tired yarn bears an unwholesome resemblance to any number of the Dick Powell-Ruby Keeler inanities manufactured across town at Warner Brothers. Frothy romantic wranglings are one thing, but Astaire and Rogers are much too sophisticated to be bothered with this nonsense about putting on a show to salvage the scuttled fishing boat once captained by Ginger's late father.

Fred and Ginger only really find themselves in this film when they cease trying to infuse some life into the plot and concentrate on the dances with their usual vigor.

*FOLLOW THE FLEET (1936).
Ginger and Fred
dancing to "Let Yourself Go"*

FOLLOW THE FLEET (1936). Fred and Ginger in a reflective mood

Adhering closely to their established ground rules, Astaire and Rogers dedicate their first number to the proposition that what begins in light-hearted competition can end with wholehearted mutual commitment. As usual, Ginger is more than willing to exhort others in song to "Let Yourself Go," but Fred has to cajole her into following her own advice. Matching wits for a synchronized tap and joining forces for an uninhibited Big Apple, Fred and Ginger vibrate with glee and proficiency, and the number is exhilarating fun.

Later on they tweak their own celebrated dance harmony with uproarious deadpan finesse during a runthrough of the Big Show to save Ginger's scow. Just for kicks, they decide to tackle "I'm Putting All My Eggs in One Basket," supposedly for the first time through, and what makes this routine so devastatingly funny is the fact that for once they are so completely out of sync with each other. Ginger is trapped in an eternal time-step while Fred is winging on to something else; Ginger swings her arms and gives Fred a slap that sends him reeling. At last linked in a waltz step, they are dumfounded when the orchestra switches to swing time. Finally, Fred unceremoniously dumps Ginger onto the floor with a sickening thud when he simply can't keep up with the chaos any longer.

Follow the Fleet peaks with their first plotted ballet, whisking them back to the swank elegance which saturated their previous efforts. In the ineffably solemn "Let's Face the Music and Dance," Fred mimes a freewheeling gambler who loses all his earnings and, on the threshold of suicide, spies a despondent Ginger contemplating a similar dire fate. After singing a throbbing chorus of the song, he dispels his own troubles by dancing Ginger out of her miseries. Similar in style to "Cheek to Cheek," this number is drenched in melancholy artifice—his outstretched arms and her arched shoulders serve as abstract symbols for psychic travail of the most exquisite kind. It would all seem a mite precious if it weren't so flawlessly executed. Here their timing is so astonishing nothing could have broken their stride—not even the fact that halfway through the sequence Ginger nearly knocked Fred unconscious with a clout from the heavily beaded sleeve of her gown.

In an attempt to convey irony, or when he finds a particular line or characterization unwieldy, Astaire occasionally gives vent to one particular vocal mannerism—a peculiar half-wheeze, half-giggle exhaled like a punctuation mark at the end of a sentence. Astaire sputters a good deal in this fashion in *Follow the Fleet,* reflecting the sense that all the raffish bonhomie required of him in this role doesn't come all that naturally. The sailor whites he affects do give him the opportunity to perform a blazing nautical tap to "I'd Rather Lead a Band," as a sort of negative image to the black-garbed title number in *Top Hat.* Yet perhaps realizing that his forte lay elsewhere, Astaire rejoined the ranks of the upper bourgeoisie for the rest of his films with Ginger; not until World War II rearranged priorities even in musicals did Fred again mingle so aggressively with the hoi polloi.

Despite its imperfections, *Follow the Fleet* enjoyed the same enthusiastic reception that had been accorded all of Astaire's efforts thus far. By 1936 Astaire had become an almost inescapable force in show business; having handily conquered the movies, toward the end of 1935 Astaire launched a successful assault on the air waves as weekly host of the nationwide Lucky Strike Hit Parade broadcasts. Despite the murderous regimen which simultaneous careers in films and radio entailed, Astaire found the challenges posed by this new medium stimulating. Late in 1936 he debuted in his own radio variety show, which achieved almost as much popular acclaim as he had won in the movies.

Nineteen thirty-six was also a memorable year in Astaire's per-

SWING TIME (1936). With Victor Moore and Ginger Rogers

sonal life, as it marked the birth of his first child, a son christened Fred, Jr. Many of his fans must have been mildly startled at his newfound fatherhood, considering that his marriage to Phyllis Potter Astaire was one of Hollywood's least publicized alliances. One aspect of stardom that Astaire genuinely abhorred was the intrusion of public curiosity into his domestic affairs, and he took great pains to separate his private life from his public image as completely as possible. And certainly, the readers of *Photoplay* and the like would have found the Astaires' private pursuits exceedingly dull copy. Extremely devoted to each other, they spent most of their spare time contentedly at home with their children or on quiet trips together. Faced with the prosaic

truth, fan-magazine sob sisters regaled their readers with yarns whose spiciness rose in inverse proportion to their basis in fact. The fans thrilled to learn that Fred and Ginger loathed each other to the point of homicide, while Phyllis Astaire harbored an insane jealousy for Fred's nimble co-star—untroubled by the obvious fact that such tidbits blithely contradicted each other.

More or less oblivious to this nonsense, Astaire girded himself for the inevitable follow-up to *Follow the Fleet*. Many familiar elements were regathered for his sixth outing with Rogers—composer Jerome Kern, lyricist Dorothy Fields, co-scenarist Allan Scott, plus Helen Broderick and Eric Blore leading the ranks of supporting players. *Swing Time* (1936) was planned as just another well-tooled diversion in the now-familiar mold, and indeed on the surface there is nothing particularly novel about the film to differentiate it from everything Astaire and Rogers had previously done. Yet *Swing Time* is a very special movie, even by Astaire's lofty standards; although perhaps less exhilarating than *Top Hat,* in a quieter, subtler way it is even more satisfying. Unlike any of their other movies, *Swing Time* combines the customary buoyancy of the Astaire-Rogers dances with the sort of resonance and intensity almost never found in such a light-hearted genre as the musical. Although the narrative thread barely holding *Swing Time* together is as flimsy as ever, in fact this film focuses on something very important indeed—namely Fred and Ginger themselves. Generally Fred and Ginger managed to infuse life into their paperweight roles only through a concentration of instinct and sheer will. Here the music summarizes and amplifies what the dramatic scenes have already made touchingly clear.

Part of the credit for this change is due director George Stevens, a newcomer to the series, fresh from the success of his sensitive *Alice Adams.* Whereas a director like Mark Sandrich merely tried to make the time pass pleasantly between songs, Stevens treats the usual Fred/Ginger spats and reconciliations with the same genuine intimacy as he had granted the rapturous delusions of Katharine Hepburn's Alice the year before. The happy result of this approach permeates the entire film. Even Astaire and his elder pal of the moment (Victor Moore, this time) do more than just exchange the usual moldy puns—they really relate to each other, with an undisguised warmth captured by none of Astaire's other films of the period.

"Chance is the fool's name for fate," went the catch phrase from *The Gay Divorcee,* and almost everything that happens in *Swing Time* is propelled by destiny disguised as mere caprice. Astaire plays "Lucky" Garnett, a vaudeville dancer/magician whose passionate interest in gambling causes him to miss his wedding to hometown sweetheart Betty Furness (who can't dance and calls him John). Subsequently he hops a freight to New York, armed with nothing but his morning suit, a toothbrush and his lucky twenty-five-cent piece, and within a few weeks has wagered his way into a sizeable bankroll. He also meets Ginger by sheer chance—they bump into each other on a crowded street—but despite the capriciousness of their meeting, Fred and Ginger are fated for each other; she teaches ballroom dancing, and as a team they soon become the darlings

SWING TIME (1936). "A Fine Romance"

of café society. More than that, Ginger brings him luck at the gaming tables, which he likes, and complements his artistry in dance, which fills an even deeper compulsion inside him.

Eventually his seemingly infallible good fortune curdles, as he nearly loses Ginger by earning enough money to live up to his promise to return home and marry Furness. Astaire vents his agony at the prospect through the calamitous threat that he's "Never Gonna Dance" again—ironically expressed by the most glorious duet they ever performed together. With classic symmetry, *Swing Time* climaxes with a wry parody of Astaire's abortive nuptials with Furness — Astaire steals the trousers of Ginger's unsavory intended, Georges Metaxa, just as his vaudeville cronies had filched Lucky's in the first reel—and the irony of seeing history repeat itself so cunningly sends everyone concerned into uncontrollable hysterics. And no other Astaire-Rogers effort concludes so enchantingly: literally on top of the world in their skyscraper aerie, Fred and Ginger delicately counterpoint "A Fine Romance" and "The Way You Look Tonight" to each other as a burst of sunlight warms the wintry New York skyline below.

In many ways the most self-consciously crafted of all Astaire's outings, *Swing Time* seamlessly combines romance and a highly tuned sense of irony, in the Kern-Fields score as well as in the dialogue. Early in the film, Fred dryly feigns incurable clumsiness so that Ginger will exhort him to "Pick Yourself Up" and learn a thing or two about terpsichore from her. After sailing weightlessly over the dance-floor railing to Ginger's enthrallment and her boss Eric Blore's pop-eyed astonishment, they are parodied in a leaden-limbed reprise by Moore and Broderick. Later, Astaire at the piano composes a paean to Ginger's loveliness, but the soft-focused vision of "The Way You Look Tonight" isn't matched by the Ginger of the evening—clothed in a sleazy wrapper, her hair swathed in shampoo. The movie's most famous song, "A Fine Romance," is even subtitled "a sarcastic love song," each complaining in sardonic rhyme of the other's deplorable lack of ardor.

Yet they redress the balance with the incomparably poignant "Never Gonna Dance," which achieves the staggering feat of recapitulating their entire relationship in five minutes of silent dance. There is something ineffable about the impact of this sequence, as it builds from a pensive side-by-side stroll to the sweeping crescendo of thwarted love which concludes it, as each fatalistically swirls up opposite

SWING TIME (1936). Dancing to "Waltz in Swing Time"

staircases toward their separate destinies. Its eloquence is such that it makes their other great *Swing Time* duet, the tinkly "Waltz in Swing Time," seem slightly pallid for all its fiendish difficulty and ethereal grace. Bleached by spotlight as they unblinkingly execute an infinity of quick waltz turns, Fred and Ginger are merely the most exquisite dancers in the world here, rather than the perfect embodiments of love as well. Only in *Swing Time* could a moment like this be surpassed by anything else.

But then Astaire tops the seemingly unsurpassable throughout *Swing Time*. Although Astaire's acting never quite lost a certain self-conscious tinge, even the smallest gesture here has the instinctive elegance which always graces Astaire the dancer—his triumphant farewell salute as he flees middle America on that freight bound for the big time, for example, or the way his arms tremble with desperation as he pleads with Ginger not to ascend that curved staircase out of his life. Although Lucky is as natty and self-confident as *Top Hat*'s Jerry Travers, the cozy wish-fulfillment world of *Swing Time* is clouded

SWING TIME (1936). As "Bojangles of Harlem"

from time to time by some recognizable daily problems, like the necessity of making money. With the character of Lucky, Astaire welded the perfect compromise between the debonair sophisticate of *Top Hat* and the more homespun heroes of *Follow the Fleet* and *Roberta*.

Blessed with a score as marvelous as this one, Astaire proves that taste and instinct have a lot more to do with delivering a song persuasively than limitless range and velvety tone. While movie tenors with more conventionally pleasing voices, like Crosby and Dick Powell, had to make do with the second-rate, the foremost popular composers vied with each other to create timeless standards for Astaire to introduce onscreen. The reason for this was pure self-interest; these songsmiths knew that more accomplished singers tended to overwhelm their work with the caramel noises emanating from their egotistical throats. They recognized that Astaire, despite the strains their songs put on his unremarkable voice, had an uncanny, dance-trained sense of tempo which shone through his singing. Incapable of the vocal embellish-

SHALL WE DANCE (1937). With Jerome Cowan and Ginger Rogers

ments his more polished rivals doted on, he could shape a touching ballad like "The Way You Look Tonight" to express the emotions and melody as simply as possible. Astaire's heretical directness as a singer made other crooners of the time seem pompous and anachronistic in comparison.

Ironically, the sequence that most clearly pointed the direction the future Astaire would take is also in some ways the most unpleasantly dated moment in *Swing Time*. Astaire intended the virtuoso "Bojangles of Harlem" as a heartfelt tribute to Bill Robinson, whom he had revered ever since appearing on the same vaudeville bill with him two decades before. The feeling behind the number is clearly genuine, and Astaire does

Robinson honor by infusing his style with a subtle suggestion of the great Robinson flash and spirit while remaining triumphantly himself. Yet the sight of Astaire in blackface remains a bit disquieting, although he completely avoids the taint of tongue-in-cheek derisiveness that usually accompanied such impersonations. Astaire felt a close affinity for jazz and the blues, and many of his subsequent films found Astaire dancing in admiring counterpoint with black dancers or incorporating their motifs into his own work. For all his naïve sincerity, such moments often seem a mite patronizing, however, albeit unintentionally so.

"Bojangles" established another, more fruitful precedent for Astaire—the use of cinematic special effects to broaden the scope of his routines. Previously, Astaire's dance sequences had been staged with almost documentary simplicity, using simple camera angles and minimal editing. "Bojangles" represented the first great Astaire number that couldn't have been approximated on the stage, climaxing with three back-projected shadows of Astaire gyrating in counterpoint to a whirling Fred/Bojangles in the foreground. It's an inspired notion dazzlingly executed, and it clearly reveals Astaire's stern determination to avoid repeating himself choreographically. This obsession with innovation deepened over the years, and trick numbers became such permanent fixtures in Astaire musicals until finally the gimmicks threatened to overwhelm Astaire's dances themselves. But in "Bojangles" the balance of footwork and hocus-pocus is perfect; *Swing Time,* apart from all its other virtues, proved that Astaire was not just a miraculous dancer, but a celluloid magician as well.

Swing Time failed to eclipse *Top Hat* at the box office—something few movies released during the Depression managed to do—but it still proved extremely popular. Since audiences had as yet shown no signs of tiring of the Fred/Ginger chemistry, Astaire found himself cast opposite Rogers for the seventh consecutive time with the

provocatively titled *Shall We Dance* (1937). RKO surrounded the pair with the accustomed team of proficient co-workers, plus arranging a long-desired reunion with George and Ira Gershwin, who had furnished the scores for two of Fred and Adele's biggest stage hits. As newcomers to the series, the Gershwins brought a welcome air of enthusiasm to *Shall We Dance,* and their songs gave the film its one true note of distinction. Yet the film is strangely dispirited; for the first time the patented Astaire-Rogers formula has become a bit rigid and perfunctory, rather than delightfully familiar. It's not just that audiences had been overexposed to it by 1937—apparently the participants had been dulled by habit as well. Although the mechanism is as well-oiled as ever, it's powered by inertia rather than inspiration.

Shall We Dance starts with an engaging premise—premier danseur Petrov (born Peter P. Peters of Pittsburgh, Pa.) falls headlong for jazzy night-club danseuse Linda Keene, and their temperaments clash until they join forces to merge ballet and tap into a new synthesis of their own. Unfortunately, this rather astute notion sinks slowly in the quicksand of indifferent plot complications. Prematurely pegged as an item in the tabloids, for the entire movie Linda and Petrov teeter between resenting each other

SHALL WE DANCE (1937).
Fred and Ginger cavort to
"Let's Call the Whole Thing Off."

It's indicative of the film's slipshod perversity that Astaire and Rogers have only one duet that really measures up to their past standards. As in their previous two films, Ginger lays the groundwork for their joint initiation with an optimistic ditty (this time the cocky "They All Laughed"). Fred baits her by pirouetting loftily around her while she fumes helplessly, until he eagerly descends to her level for one of their cheeriest and most varied tap sessions. Subsequently they exchange their tap shoes for roller skates and a musical sprint in Central Park to "Let's Call the Whole Thing Off," but however delightful this sounds in theory, behind that gritted smile Ginger has to concentrate too hard on keeping her balance to exude the requisite air of impromptu grace. And the climactic title number is hardly a duet at all, for all its eerie surrealism, as Fred darts frantically about in search of the real Ginger buried somewhere in a sea of chorus girls sporting identical waxen Ginger masks. Astaire's haunting version of "They Can't Take That Away From Me" would have provided the perfect accompaniment for one of those somberly erotic interludes they do so well, but instead he squanders the moment with a ballerina-impersonating contortionist (Harriet Hoctor), whose specialty was to bend herself into a human croquet wicket

and the web of phony publicity that has linked them, and allowing the inevitable to take its course. It was a revered Astaire-Rogers convention for Ginger to spend the first few reels of every effort fuming at Fred's cheekiness, but here her irritation is so arbitrary and prolonged that for the first time one wonders why Astaire should bother with anyone as capricious and petty as she is.

SHALL WE DANCE (1937). Fred dances with the "real" Ginger.

and kick herself in the head as she advanced toward the dumbstruck camera.

The ironic result was that most of the memorable moments in *Shall We Dance* are sung rather than choreographed. The Gershwins admirably fill the obligatory slot for an Astaire-Rogers bickering patter song with "Let's Call the Whole Thing Off," which has little relevance to the moment in which it's spotted in the story, but everything to do with Fred and Ginger's four-year relationship to that point. Throughout *Shall We Dance*, large bodies of water bring out the romantic urge in Astaire.

During an Atlantic crossing he corners Ginger at the boat railing to woo her with the blithe "Beginner's Luck," while a fog-shrouded ferry in New York harbor sets the scene for the more plaintive "They Can't Take That Away From Me." Each brings out different facets of Astaire's unerring way with a song, and they provide most of the film's few unadulterated pleasures.

Under the Slavic nom de danse, Astaire/Peters is his usual hearty, unpretentious self, who can't help bursting into a time step even when he's supposed to be practicing his pliés. Astaire wryly milks his phony ethnicity for all its comic possibili-

A DAMSEL IN DISTRESS (1937). With Joan Fontaine

ties, particularly when he transforms himself into a road-company Boris Goudonov in order to meet Ginger's expectations of him as a barrel-voiced Russian egomaniac. Yet in private he reverts to type at the first convenient moment, and "Slap That Bass," his biggest solo turn, owes much more to *Swing Time* than it does to *Swan Lake*. On a set that looks like God's power generator, he amuses a group of bass-playing black engine stokers in tapped syncopation with the chugging and whirring of the ship's machinery. "Slap That Bass" scintillates, and so does Astaire for most of *Shall We Dance,* but the vitality that once surged through the team had ebbed considerably by this point.

RKO quickly heeded the signals and offered the pair a temporary respite from each other, assigning Rogers to *Stage Door* and Astaire to *A Damsel in Distress* (1937). Both agreed eagerly to this trial separation, although Astaire really risked a good deal more in the bargain. While Ginger had successfully alternated the Astaire musicals with straight dramatic vehicles opposite other leading men, since attaining stardom Astaire had never dallied once with anyone but Rogers, with or without music. (In the minds of some of his admirers, that would have been tantamount to adultery.) *A Damsel in Distress* sought to avoid unnecessary comparisons with the Astaire-Rogers efforts by casting Fred opposite

72

someone as unlike Ginger as possible; hence the script called for said damsel to be English, somewhat demure, and impeccably well-bred. Preliminary choice Ruby Keeler certainly couldn't have gotten more demure if she tried, but being neither British nor, heaven knows, aristocratic, she was rejected for the role. The superb Jessie Matthews matched all the prerequisites, but she was making too much money as the dancing idol of the British screen to be bothered with a trek to Hollywood. In obvious desperation RKO scanned their roster of featured players and came up with an obscure starlet named Joan Fontaine, who was sort of English, very inexpensive and absolutely no threat to anyone, much less the memory of Ginger, when it came to dancing.

With Ginger or without, the Astaire-RKO musicals always told intoxicating fables meant for credulous grown-ups, but *A Damsel in Distress* carried this trend one step further. As the title indicates, *Damsel* is a literal medieval fairytale translated into knowing thirties' vernacular, parodying the clichés of the genre while reveling in all of its madcap variations on the hoary theme. The hapless Fontaine plays one Lady Alyce, confined to the tower of her family's ancestral digs for promising her hand to some unsuitable American chap, while Astaire finds greatness suddenly thrust upon him as the dashing gallant drafted to extricate her ladyship from this predicament. Our hero and heroine are joined by the regulation assortment of potty English eccentrics, including an elderly lord of the manor, (Montagu Love) who is too busy mulching his roses to trouble himself with family intrigue, and his nerve-wracked dowager sister (Constance Collier), for whom time apparently stopped sometime prior to the War of the Roses.

Yet for all its antique shenanigans, *Damsel* is almost aggressively contemporary. The lady in question makes merry in amusement parks and drives a convertible, presumably paid for by all those tourists whose sixpences keep the castle financially above moat level. For all his athletic bravado, Astaire's swashbuckling swain is just an American swing hoofer on the lam from his rabid female fans, accompanied by a hardboiled press agent (George Burns) and a scramble-brained secretary (Gracie Allen). The Gershwin score sets the tone for this *moderne* Anglo-Saxon tale—Lady Alyce's blue-blooded suitor (Ray Noble) forsakes the classics for a wacky snippet of hide-ho, while three of the manor's madrigal singers harmonize to "Nice Work If You Can Get It" like a sort of catatonic Boswell Sisters. To make the revolution complete, Astaire shatters a staid

A DAMSEL IN DISTRESS (1937). With Gracie Allen and George Burns

formal gathering with a torrid drum solo, kicking the daylights out of the instruments while spiraling around the floor to the meter of his frenzied feet.

Even when he isn't dancing, Astaire is an object lesson in perpetual motion throughout *A Damsel in Distress*. Instead of slaying his dragons, Astaire simply runs in the opposite direction —from female groupies, irate constables, obstinate valets, Lady Alyce's snooty relations, and even at times Lady Alyce herself. He breaks his stride just long enough for a contemplative stroll through Alyce's grounds, proclaiming his romantic good fortune in "A Foggy Day in London Town" as a shaft of day-for-night moonbeams penetrates the darkness. But this lapse is only temporary—before long he is

leaping from Fontaine's stone parapet, swinging like Tarzan from branch to branch before landing unscathed on terra firma.

Yet Astaire's hyperactivity and director George Stevens' brisk tempo don't completely camouflage the fact that something very crucial is missing from *A Damsel in Distress*. One of the joys of any satisfying Astaire musical rests in the warm intimacy he achieves with a suitable vis-á-vis, which the pallid Fontaine of 1937 emphatically was not. At this embryonic stage of her career, Fontaine was extremely pretty but she hadn't the remotest idea of how to handle comedy. More crucially, it seems a complete betrayal of Astaire's screen persona for him to fall for someone who absolutely can't dance. In recognition of her limitations, Fontaine partners Astaire only once. Yet "Things Are Looking Up" only magnifies her defects; she would have had enough trouble negotiating her way across the smooth surface of a ballroom floor, but here she has to scramble over an obstacle course of rocks and rills in a riotously unconvincing display of gazelle-like abandon.

To compensate, the film shifts its focus from Astaire's romantic pursuits to the familiar but most welcome antics of Burns and Allen. Apart from George's wry composure and Gracie's breathlessly adenoidal nonsequiturs, Burns and Allen also display a surprising aptitude for choreographed clowning with Fred. The three of them dust each other with whisk brooms before engaging three vicious suits of armor in merry battle, with delightful results. Better yet is their danced exploration of a wondrous amusement park-playland — shimmying before trick mirrors, high-stepping across moving sidewalks, and sliding precipitously down polished chutes, accompanied by screeches of glee from Gracie.

Abetted by George, Gracie, and the Gershwins, Astaire strives mightily to enliven the movie and the exquisite photographic use of natural outdoor locales (most unusual for an Astaire musical) makes *Damsel* the most beautiful of all Astaire's films of the period to look at, save possibly *Swing Time*. Still, the film was Astaire's first to fare poorly at the box office, at the same time that *Stage Door*'s tumultuous popularity with fans and critics alike proved anew that Ginger could thrive very nicely without him. Astaire's solo prestige declined further when an exhibitors' ad appearing in the *Independent Film Journal* proclaimed such luminaries as Mae West, Katharine Hepburn, Marlene Dietrich, Joan Crawford, and himself to be "box office poison." RKO's response was to play safe and reteam him with Rogers; Astaire remained temporarily idle while Ginger fulfilled her commitments to star in *Vivacious Lady* and *Having Wonderful Time* without him.

Carefree provided the occasion for their reluctant reunion, and never was a film more inappropriately titled—something like *Down to Earth* would have been much more apt. *Shall We Dance* had shown definite signs of impending trouble in the Astaire-Rogers paradise, so *Carefree* transplanted them into the more prosaic milieu of typical thirties middle-class farce, punctuated infrequently by Fred's and Ginger's inimitable musical flights of fantasy. Usually Astaire's movie world looked like nowhere else on earth or on screen; here he lives and works in the usual Hollywood-backlot facsimile of Manhattan, finding diversion in what looks like an honest-to-God

CAREFREE (1938). With Ginger Rogers and Walter Kingsford

country club where real mortals could be expected to congregate. Moreover, for all the farcical treatment it gets, *Carefree's* main theme—psychoanalysis—poses a somber contrast to the frivolous baubles that usually passed for plots in Astaire films.

Within this more naturalistic context, Astaire and Rogers both give most persuasive performances, and the film has more than its share of amusing and touching moments. Yet *Carefree* did more than provide the inevitable change of pace for Fred and Ginger—it stripped them of many of those mythic qualities that had made their teaming so unique. Superficially much less trivial than its predecessors, *Carefree* is also much less memorable. Removed from their special

universe, here Astaire and Rogers seem like two accomplished pros who happen to work well together, rather than the sublime inevitability of yore.

For the first time neither a bandleader nor a professional dancer, Astaire plays a rather dour psychiatrist whose clientele abounds with an assortment of what he refers to as pampered, maladjusted females. Rogers joins the ranks of his patients because she keeps balking at the altar and doesn't know why. (Considering that her fiancé is Ralph Bellamy, eternal stooge of thirties' screwball comedy, this is actually a sure sign of sanity on Ginger's part.) When Astaire persuades her to air her subconscious, she begins to dream of her suave analyst rather than her supposed beloved. Out of loyalty to Bellamy, Astaire hypnotizes Rogers into loathing Fred and adoring her fiancé, until the good doctor's own subconscious asserts itself, and he toils desperately to snap her out of the spell he has woven all too successfully.

Remnants of the old Astaire-Rogers pattern still cling to *Carefree*, and as usual their three dance duets are geared to evoke the emotional progression of their relationship—often more eloquently, in fact, than the dialogue they utter in the interim. But *Carefree* really reflects Rogers' attempt to be taken seriously as a distinctive actress-comedienne in her own right, rather than as Astaire's eternally dutiful if backward dancing apprentice. This time Ginger is the aggressor in their relationship, and it is she who becomes obsessed with the notion of dancing with him, rather than the usual other way around. Playing a decorous heroine with untapped libidinal resources, Rogers gets to alternate poignant restraint and freewheeling rambunctiousness with admirable facility, while Astaire watches calmly from the sidelines.

As the man who unleashes Ginger's inhibitions, Astaire applies his usual smooth charm only as a phony sort of bedside manner to cajole his recalcitrant patient. Portraying a psychiatrist, even in musical comedy, represses Astaire's customary ebullience—in *Carefree* he is rather solemn, and suddenly seems much older than in any of his previous films. He furthermore adds a new note of misogyny to his facade of professional aloofness; thanks to his female patients, Astaire categorizes women, including Ginger, as spoiled, fatuous creatures until he allows emotion to break through all those rational defenses. Astaire handles this rather abrupt shift in his screen persona most sensitively; the hushed resignation with which he brainwashes the hypnotized Ginger is perhaps the most moving bit of acting he had done to that point. Vestiges of this character reappeared frequently as Astaire got older, and many Astaire movies later focused on his eleventh-hour realization that he cares for the woman who has been subtly pursuing him from their first meeting. "Why didn't you tell me that I was in love with you?" inquires Astaire of Judy Garland in *Easter Parade* ten years later. The question could just as well have been applied by Fred to the Ginger Rogers of *Carefree*.

One of the things that made Astaire and Rogers so special as a couple was that each so obviously fulfilled a compelling need in the other, at least once they started to dance. In *Carefree*, Astaire gives repressed Ginger something wonderful to dream about, while

CAREFREE (1938). Doing "the Yam"

she gives vitality to his heretofore passionless life. Eroticism invades a slumbering Rogers when Astaire serenades her in her dreams with "I Used to Be Color-Blind," as they leap in slow-motion over a collection of enormous lilypads. The undemonstrative Astaire lets loose on the golf course (a favorite offscreen haunt) with "Since They Turned 'Loch Lomond' into Swing," smashing drives with abandoned precision only because Ginger's scoffing has goaded him into doing so.

Later he sheds his reserve forever, thanks to Rogers' persuasive powers, to the rhythm of "The Yam," unfortunately one of Irving Berlin's more inane lyrics. Loping from room to room like syncopated Pied Pipers to the country club set, Fred and Ginger enliven this not very novel specialty dance step with their exhilarating good spirits, concluding their travels with that astonishing moment in which Astaire props his leg on a succession of white-clothed tables as Rogers effortlessly sails over him.

"I Used to Be Color-Blind," although a much more sophisticated Berlin song, is rather less perfectly realized onscreen. The slow-motion effect seems unnecessary and detracts from the sensuality of the already languid choreography, and the number cries out for Technicolor—the lyrics list practically every tint in the spectrum, and the fanciful backdrop of waterlilies and such looks awfully tatty in black and white.

Yet their dance accompaniment to "Change Partners" is so magnificent that all by itself it redeems the film's other disappointments. On some level Astaire had often hypnotized Ginger into revealing unexpected facets of herself in the dance, but "Change Partners" makes Astaire's mesmeric effect on her achingly explicit. Usually Astaire thwarts her reluctance to dance by physically blocking her attempted exit, but having placed her under a trance for the moment, here Astaire draws Rogers toward him without even touching her at first—his hands jerk toward her and her supple body glides to his bidding. She stands mute and motionless while Fred ponders each subsequent move, until once more his arms pulsate with some abstract choreographed command for Ginger to dance into life. In one particularly electric moment, Ginger glides backward toward a beckoning Fred, although she hasn't seen his gestures at all—her back was turned to him the whole time. It is really as though some invisible magnetic force inexorably draws them together. Gorgeously choreographed and performed with staggering finesse, "Change Partners" is a tribute to the perfec-

CAREFREE (1938). Dancing to "Change Partners"

THE STORY OF VERNON AND IRENE CASTLE (1939).
Courting Irene on a park bench

tion with which their bodies and temperaments complement each other.

Carefree's relatively lukewarm reception at the box office confirmed what everyone involved had long suspected; the beloved saga of Astaire and Rogers was living on borrowed time. To give the waning team a memorable send-off, the studio hit upon an inspired notion; in *The Story of Vernon and Irene Castle* (1939), Astaire and Rogers summed up their own blazing partnership by reincarnating the legendary dance team of the previous generation. Certainly no one could have filled the shoes of

the Castles on screen as completely as Astaire and Rogers, and *Vernon and Irene Castle* proved in many respects to be their most ambitious project. Their first period effort, this film featured a story more complex than their usual charades of mistaken identity and misplaced emotions, characterizations that required more than their usual patina of starry charm, and dance routines in which their own distinctive styles had to be submerged to recreate steps patented by someone else. Moreover, *Vernon and Irene Castle* rejects the humorous tone that had characterized everything from *Flying Down to Rio* even through *Carefree*. In retelling an essentially tragic story of meteoric triumph followed by untimely death, the film is about as jocular as *The Grapes of Wrath*.

Supervised by the very perspicacious Irene Castle, the film adheres more closely than most movie biographies to the restraints of factual accuracy. At their first encounter, Vernon is a successful comic second banana on Broadway, while Irene is a perky adolescent with starry-eyed aspirations for a dancing career. Vernon deserts comedy for a dance act with Irene, and after their marriage they face an abortive audition in New York and further hard times in France before galvanizing Paris overnight with such novel steps as the Castle Walk. America embraces them with even greater hysteria, as the entire nation imitates their clothes, their dances, and even Irene's revolutionary short-bobbed hair. (Reportedly the real Mrs. Castle threw a holy fit when Ginger refused to trim her curls accordingly, and indeed her make-up and coiffure are the only really anachronistic touches in the film.) With the outbreak of World War I in 1914, the patriotic Vernon enlists as a flyer. Following a series of perilous missions against the Germans, he is ironically killed on a routine flight exercise in Texas.

All this is told with genuine tenderness and considerable restraint, heightened undoubtedly by Astaire and Rogers' belief that they would probably never work together again. Yet for all its warmth, *Vernon and Irene Castle* falls prey to the same malady that afflicted most films of its ilk. Desperate not to malign the memories of the dead or the sensibilities of the living, such portraits of ex-theatrical greats generally filtered out every character foible that might have made these figures really intriguing as screen subjects, much less believable as human beings. Unsurprisingly, director H. C. Potter surrounds these people with the expected aura of canonization. As depicted here, the Castles are so gifted, so stoical at the threat of heartbreak, so unrelievedly devoted to each other, and ultimately so much more tedious than the flawed and lively fictional characters Astaire and Rogers had played in the past.

As with *Carefree*, this film caters more expressly to Ginger's burgeoning dramatic aspirations than to Astaire's customary strengths, but curiously enough he comes off the better of the two by not trying so stridently to impress with virtuoso acting technique. Rogers has her share of poignant moments, but on the whole she tends to rise a bit too self-consciously to the occasion—all freckles and adenoids as the teen-aged heroine (one of Rogers' favorite affectations), a

THE STORY OF VERNON AND IRENE CASTLE (1939).
Doing "the Castle Walk"

THE STORY OF VERNON AND IRENE CASTLE (1939).
Their last waltz together

studied portrait of shrill concern as wifely Irene, panic-stricken at Vernon's heedless determination to do his bit for the war effort. Astaire's fundamental nonchalance onscreen frees him from such tricky mannerisms, and he inhabits his role with much less obvious strain than Rogers does hers. Now forty years old, Astaire's irrepressible dynamism has gained an appealing calmness at its core, which makes Vernon's solicitude toward Irene and his brave indifference to danger unaffectedly moving.

Astaire and Rogers' painstaking reproductions of the Castles' most famed routines glow with exuberance and display their astonishing versatility as dancers in full measure. The choreography runs the gamut from the brisk one-step of "Too Much Mustard," featuring a lightning-quick series of fast twirls, to an exquisitely simple waltz, illustrating Vernon and Irene's reunion during the war at the scene of their first Parisian triumph. In between, they perform a montage of steps to sum up their swift rise to fame, including the Maxixe, the Castle Polka, and a faintly ludicrous tango, featuring Astaire clad in black satin bell-bottoms, climaxing with the film's cleverest image—Fred and Ginger cavorting across a gargantuan map of the United States, as ant-like swarms of dance devotees spring up in their wake. Astaire also introduces the film's one original song, the attractive ballad "Only When You're in My Arms," and executes two solo dances with great dash.

The trouble with most of these routines is that sprightly as they are, they lack the spontaneity and emotional resonance that marked Fred and Ginger's earlier work; the tricky, formalized patterns they re-create here are technically impressive but not much more than that. In a way, Fred and Ginger are really too good to do the Castles justice. By the evidence presented in the film, the Castles were trendsetters to be sure, but basically just a pair of unusually graceful and clever performers, while the great Astaire-Rogers routines are far greater than the sum of their dancing parts. Hemmed in by biographical fidelity, Astaire hasn't the leeway he needs to weave his usual dance fabric of mood and emotion.

Compared to the exhilarating poetry of Astaire's great vehicles with Rogers, *The Story of Vernon and Irene Castle* is fairly earthbound prose. Yet as the farewell chapter to this extraordinary series, it evokes the perfect note of nostalgia and melancholy. Consciously or not, *Vernon and Irene Castle* really narrates the history of Astaire and Rogers, down to Irene/Ginger's transition to dramatic film stardom once deprived of her husband/partner. The Castles were only more fortunate than the actors that played them, in that Vernon died before the Castles could outgrow each other, as Ginger and Fred had done before our eyes. The movie closes with the haunting shot of a ghostly Vernon and Irene pirouetting down a garden path into infinity, but the poignance it evokes has little to do with any emotion we have come to feel for the Castles in the previous ninety minutes. Astaire and Rogers themselves dissolve into memory in that moment; she to win an Oscar the following year for her ode to the white-collar girl, *Kitty Foyle,* he to face an uncertain future wandering free-lance from studio to studio in the quest for a rejuvenated career. Once before Astaire had managed to defeat the odds and forge a career on his own; now faced with Ginger's defection, Astaire had returned to square one in search of a new miracle.

With his RKO contract expired and no new long-term prospects on the horizon, Astaire carefully sifted his options for the future. After a leisurely European voyage with his wife, he returned to Hollywood to accept MGM's offer to team up with the studio's queen of terpsichore, Eleanor Powell, for the latest of her *Broadway Melody* extravaganzas. At the time, *Broadway Melody of 1940* must have looked like a promising solution to Astaire's career doldrums, but the result proved emphatically otherwise. The mediocre final entry in a series that had been pretty undistinguished to begin with, *Broadway Melody* surrounded Astaire with a menagerie of grotesque specialty acts, stifled his usual brashness with an inferiority complex, and thrust him into the spotlight with a partner whose style clashed discordantly with his own.

Four screenwriters labored over the scenario for this *Broadway Melody*, and their combined toils wrought just another soggy backstage saga containing the most unsuitable role for Astaire since the distant days of *Flying Down to Rio*. As the less arrogant half of a struggling dance act with George Murphy, Astaire gets to languish with unrequited yearnings as his erstwhile partner makes time with Broadway star Powell and cops the career break that had been meant for Astaire. Eventually, of course,

NOT HEP TO THAT STEP

hubris hits the cocky George with a flourish and Astaire gains both stardom and his beloved, but by then the damage had already been done. Divested of most of his usual vigor and optimism, Astaire suffers visibly from having to feign passive martyrdom in such massive doses. He spends much of his screen time casting mournful glances out of camera range, presumably in search of all those RKO artisans who knew how to showcase him properly.

When he isn't dodging such gruesome diversions as a girl juggler who balances balls with what looks like a drug-store vibrator jammed in her mouth, Astaire finds some respite in the uneven Cole Porter score. At various moments he smoothly fences a phlegmatic Murphy with his walking stick to Porter's "Don't Monkey with Broadway", and later launches into a jazzy display of what he referred to in *Roberta* as "feelthy piano" for a snappy paean to Powell's charms with "I've Got My Eyes On You." Interestingly, Astaire's most convincing display of affection toward his co-star takes place while she is discreetly offcamera. Powell's steely grin and wooden line readings deflate any emotion that the

BROADWAY MELODY OF 1940
(1940). With George Murphy

BROADWAY MELODY OF 1940
(1940). Dancing to "I Concentrate
On You" with Eleanor Powell

dialogue might have contained, but what's worse, her approach to dance is the antithesis of Astaire's, consisting of lots of flash but no substance or feeling.

Powell is really most at home as the human slingshot tossed about by a bevy of sailor-suited chorus boys in her "I Am the Captain" production number. While Astaire minimized gimmicks to create a smooth momentum for his routines, Powell shoves everything else to the background to show off her high kicks and pneumatic-drilled tap prowess. Unlike Rogers, Powell had very definite choreographic notions of her own, and she drags Astaire down with her into the velvety kitsch of the "I Concentrate On You" ballet, as they twitter about the stage in masks and harlequin costumes worthy of a

BROADWAY MELODY OF 1940 (1940). Dancing to "Begin the Beguine" with Eleanor Powell

Radio City Corps de Ballet April Fool's Day Pageant. It is as though Astaire had abandoned Ginger for the likes of another Harriet Hoctor.

Yet there was no denying Powell's blinding facility with a tap routine, and their long climactic duet to "Begin the Beguine" is soaringly effective. Whirling like pinwheels around each other and tapping out messages in swing-rhythmed code, Astaire and Powell shimmer with expertise and belatedly manage to charge *Broadway Melody* and their own teamwork with vitality. Astaire has a delightfully unexpected effect on Powell in this number—following Fred's example, for once she is not just intent on "killing the people" with her leggy precision, but she actually seems to be enjoying herself as well, and it makes all the difference in her work.

The dissonant *Broadway Melody* failed to cause any stampede at the box-office, but at the very least it had indisputably been a major effort that somehow failed to live up to expectations. Unfortunately no such claim could have been made for the dismal *Second Chorus* (1940), Astaire's immediate follow-up to *Broadway Melody*. An inexpensive independent production released through Paramount, *Se-*

cond Chorus compounds the flaws of its tacky production values and undistinguished score by casting Astaire adrift in a role more suited to the likes of Mickey Rooney. Through some incredible feat of illogic, he and Burgess Meredith portray slightly overage collegians who spend the entire film playing sophomoric pranks on each other while competing for Paulette Goddard's heart and a job with Artie Shaw's swing band. Predictably, Astaire's desperate attempt to grapple with a role two decades too young for him and completely alien to his gifts proves much funnier than the limp practical jokes and sodden quips provided for him in the script.

Reflecting the shifting musical tastes of America's moviegoing bobbysoxers, *Second Chorus* soft-pedals Astaire's dancing talents in order to showcase the more timely allure of Artie Shaw's big-band sound. Astaire equably tries to adapt to the new order of things, taking a few game licks at a jazz trumpet and colloquially informing the hepcats in the audience, "I Ain't Hep to That Step But I'll Dig It." The Shaw brass and the Astaire class do combine success-

SECOND CHORUS (1940). With Paulette Goddard

SECOND CHORUS (1940). *Dancing with Paulette Goddard*

YOU'LL NEVER GET RICH (1941). With Rita Hayworth and chorus

YOU'LL NEVER GET RICH (1941). With Rita Hayworth

fully for the finale; leading the Shaw combo in the bandleader's "Swing Concerto," Astaire substitutes a conductor's baton for his trusty cane as he crouches and swirls to the homogenized jazz orchestrations, miming a fevered drum solo and tapping and trumpeting simultaneously for an upbeat finish.

Like Joan Fontaine, Paulette Goddard lacked the basic prerequisites for partnering Astaire in dance, but at least her matter-of-fact pertness provides a refreshing antidote for the adolescent boisterousness imposed on her co-stars. Spurning the onscreen advances of future real-life husband Meredith, she joins Astaire for one energetic jitterbug in which her vivacity more than compensates for her sketchy technique. But the absence of an ideal musical companion was the least of Astaire's problems in *Second Chorus*. Its deserved failure with the public accelerated the decline that had been evident since *A Damsel in Distress*. Conceivably, another low-budget fiasco like *Second Chorus* might have banished Astaire from the screen indefinitely.

Fortunately, an unlikely Fairy Godmother named Harry Cohn propitiously rescued Astaire from this dire prospect. Cohn's domain at Columbia was relatively humble by Hollywood standards, but it possessed one great potential asset —a beauteous ex-dancer named Rita Hayworth, who was then hovering on the verge of major stardom. As her dramatic abilities were decidedly limited at that point, the studio decided to promote Hayworth's attributes in a series of musicals, with a prestigious assist from established pro Astaire. At first, Astaire hesitated; he had known Hayworth's heel-clicking father Eduardo Cansino from their long-gone vaudeville days, and feared inviting ridicule by romancing the considerably younger Hayworth to music. Nevertheless, he eventually signed to do two films with Hayworth, which turned out to be the wisest career decision he had made since parting from Ginger and RKO two years before.

In terms of budget and scope *You'll Never Get Rich* (1941) is decidedly on the modest side, but its spirit and assurance turn the film's unpretentiousness into a decided asset. In its plebeian way just as fantasy-laden as Astaire's deco dreams at RKO, the film recognizes the coming war by replacing Astaire's dress whites with olive drab for the duration. As a musical-comedy director happily joining the army to avoid the seeming wiles of chorine Rita and the bumbling machinations of producer Robert Benchley, Astaire spends most of his time in T-shirts and army fatigues, while breaking up maneuvers with an irresistible buck-and-wing.

In keeping with its recruitment-poster aspirations, the movie takes place in an army post which resembles nothing so much as a summer camp for mischievous boy scouts. For such minor misdeeds as impersonating an officer while AWOL, Astaire gets slapped on the wrist with a few days in a cozy brig furnished with a contingent of bluesy black soldiers who while away their time accompanying Fred for his irrepressible military tap exercises. Eventually his kindly commanding officers spring him from his soft confinement so he can entertain the troops and woo the recalcitrant Rita (whom Astaire had misjudged in civilian life), and he even gets time off for a brief honeymoon with his dancing bride. Director Sidney Lanfield's refusal to take one moment of this nonsense seriously gives the film its properly light-hearted tone, and the whole thing afforded Astaire an invigorating change of pace from his fraternity-row antics in *Second Chorus*.

Though Cole Porter never composed quite as effectively for the screen as for the stage, his contributions to *You'll Never Get Rich* are eminently serviceable, and provide the excuse for Astaire's most

YOU WERE NEVER LOVELIER (1942). Prancing about Adolphe Menjou's office

varied workout in some time. While still in civvies, he alternates between soaring semi-ballet and blistering tap as he guides opposing armies of rehearsing chorus girls in the "Boogie Barcarolle." and bids them a fond farewell at Grand Central Station with a Cohan-like strut, proclaiming, "I'm Shooting the Works for Uncle Sam." In uniform he shakes the guardhouse rafters with "Since I Kissed My Baby Goodbye", a sprightly jumble of athletic jumps, military salutes, and regulation tapping footwork.

His two full-scale duets with Hayworth range from a rhumba-flavored outing in deference to her Latin origins to "So Near and Yet So Far," Porter's brightest song in the score, and a jive-ridden tap competition for a high-spirited martial finale entitled "The Wedding Cake-walk". Neither quite as expressive as Rogers nor as limber-jointed as Eleanor Powell, as a dancer Hayworth's greatest asset is her light-hearted sensuousness, which nicely counterbalances Astaire's supple asceticism. *You'll Never Get Rich* pleasantly fulfilled Columbia's expectations, propelling Hayworth closer to genuine stardom while shoring up Astaire's popularity with the mass audience.

While *You'll Never Get Rich* at least had pretensions to topicality, *You Were Never Lovelier* (1942), is unabashedly drenched in fairy-tale escapism. Set in a palms-and-orchids postcard reproduction of Buenos Aires, the film's narrative even outdoes *You'll Never Get Rich* for unadulterated flimsiness. It has something to do with stern Argentine paterfamilias Adolphe Menjou's search for a mystery suitor to woo iceberg Hayworth out of her romantic fantasies so that her younger sisters will be finally free to marry. William Seiter's directorial sluggishness regrettably hadn't been enlivened by the passage of time since *Roberta,* and the film almost succumbs to the accumulated weight of its needless plot twists, Menjou's eternal tantrums, and several coagulating infusions of Xavier Cugat and his band.

Fortunately Astaire's suave footwork, Hayworth's loveliness, and a particularly lilting Jerome Kern-Johnny Mercer score combine to restore the proper balance. Astaire delivers a virtual reprise of his *Damsel in Distress* performance as the vacationing dancer drafted to arouse the dormant emotions of the highborn heroine, lamely protesting all the while that he has traveled all that distance to relax and play the horses—not, heaven forfend, to dance. True to his word, Astaire keeps the audience waiting for an unconscionably long time before letting loose with a Latin-with-a-vengeance, hip-swaying journey through Menjou's office, indulging his penchant for percus-

YOU WERE NEVER LOVELIER (1942). With Rita Hayworth

sion by knocking on wood (a desk, a lamp, a table, Menjou's skull) in syncopated counterpoint to his footwork.

In proper Sleeping Beauty fashion, Hayworth self-consciously wades through all those lines she has to read, only to blossom exuberantly at Astaire's touch on the dance floor. Their romantic duets harken back in mood to Astaire's erotic turns with Ginger, but Hayworth's lush voluptuousness tends to overwhelm Astaire's spindly frame in these cheek-to-cheek interludes—he can't quite ease Hayworth aloft with the same effortless air as he did the more streamlined Rogers.

Much more effective is their saddle-shoed, side-by-side boogie-woogie to "The Shorty George." Though composer Kern is clearly ill-at-ease with the song's black bebopper rhythms, Astaire and Hayworth perform it delectably, parodying the eccentricities of forties' jivers while reveling in the jitterbugging joy of their steps. Their bow-off is particularly witty; clutching at each other like moonstruck bobbysoxers, Fred and Rita blissfully gaze heavenward as they slowly wriggle their bottoms toward the wings. Yet despite this, Astaire's most memorable moment in the film isn't choreographed at all; hired early into the film to entertain at the wedding of Rita's older sister, Astaire softly caresses the ballad "Dearly Beloved" in his inimitably hushed quaver.

Astaire interrupted his revels with Hayworth at Bing Crosby's request to join forces at Paramount for *Holiday Inn* (1942). Paradoxically, this film proved to be Astaire's most accomplished effort since he left RKO, while bearing grim omens concerning his uncertain future as a major film star in his own right. If anything, Irving Berlin's melodic score and Mark Sandrich's glossy helming outshine their contributions to *Carefree,* their last collaboration with Astaire. However, Paramount housed Crosby under a long-term contract, and in any event he was a much more potent force at the box-office in 1942 than Astaire was; hence, *Holiday Inn* was constructed along the lines of the usual easygoing Crosby entries. While the singer dominates the story, croons the most prominent tunes, and wins the more desirable leading lady, Astaire contents himself with his usual handful of blithe dances and the essentially thankless role of second banana to the real star of this enterprise.

As *Holiday Inn* opens, singer-composer Crosby and hoofer Astaire vie for the affections of unworthy colleague Virginia Dale, only to see their act collapse when Crosby opts for the bucolic peace of Holiday Inn, a farm which he plans to open for revelers on holiday weekends. He is joined in this enterprise by the suitably demure Marjorie Reynolds, whom Fred also pursues after Virginia has ditched him to wallow in oil with a Texas millionaire. The expected rivalry fiercely ensues, but although Fred and Hollywood temporarily lure Marjorie away from Crosby, he asserts his top-billing prerogatives to gain her back; as an afterthought, Virginia Dale is yanked back on to console Astaire, just in time for the finale.

This divertingly inconsequential plot neatly meshes with the Berlin songs, cued to coincide with the appropriate holidays: "Be Careful, It's My Heart" (Valentine's Day), "Easter Parade," "I've Plenty to Be Thankful For" (Thanksgiving), and naturally, Crosby's poignant classic, "White Christmas." Made very shortly after Pearl Harbor, *Holiday Inn* only fleetingly reflects the ominous wartime climate; while Crosby solemnly intones Berlin's "Song of Freedom," a Paramount newsreel informs the audience that America is all about munitions factories, guns, ships, and planes, at least for the duration.

Compared to the other studios where Astaire had toiled, Para-

HOLIDAY INN (1942). With Marjorie Reynolds and Bing Crosby

HOLIDAY INN (1942). Fred "says it" with firecrackers.

mount was notably short on distinctive female dancers. (Crosby heroines only needed to simper convincingly.) *Holiday Inn* was no exception to this long-standing tradition, and throughout Astaire alternates between the interchangeably bland Marjorie Reynolds and Virginia Dale. He floats in waltz time around a huge paper valentine with Reynolds, struggles to maintain his composure in wigs and satin as Crosby's band capriciously interrupts their Washington's Birthday minuet with a blast of jive, and persuades Dale in a song that "You're Easy to Dance With," and proving it with a spirited dance chorus.

Each of these numbers sparkles with the cold glint of expertise, but deprived of a really individual partner like Rogers or Hayworth, Astaire works best when he works alone. A smoldering cigarette and a box of firecrackers provide the inspiration for Astaire's *Holiday Inn* highlight, as he casually combines the two in explosive, earsplitting counterpoint to his scorching footwork for his Independence Day homage, "Say It with Fireworks." As in all his most stunning routines, Astaire makes the most complicated steps look incredibly easy, the spontaneous result of quick-witted imagination and sheer emotional exuberance.

THE SKY'S THE LIMIT (1943). With Robert Ryan (seated)

Yet for all Astaire's dynamic bursts of choreographed energy, *Holiday Inn* reverberates mostly to the slower pulse of Crosby's vibrato, and its popularity enhanced Crosby's career far more than it did Astaire's. In any case, Astaire's proudest achievement in 1942 was neither the success of *Holiday Inn* nor *You Were Never Lovelier,* but rather the birth of his daughter Ava.

The following year Astaire returned to leading-man status at his old haven RKO for *The Sky's the Limit,* and discovered that conditions had changed drastically since his departure after *Vernon and Irene Castle.* As the studio's foremost attraction some years before, Astaire had been accorded ample budgets, lavish backdrops glisteningly photographed, a full complement of original songs, and Ginger Rogers to dance with. *The Sky's the Limit* reflected wartime austerity and Astaire's relative decline through its drab production values, meager folio of just three Harold Arlen tunes, and the uninspiring choice of Joan Leslie to play opposite him.

The film's primary asset at the time was its wartime topicality. Once more in uniform, Astaire portrays a heroic Flying Tiger on leave who pursues magazine photographer Leslie to the consternation of her amorous publisher Robert Benchley and the amusement of

THE SKY'S THE LIMIT (1943).
With Joan Leslie

Fred's copilot pal, Robert Ryan. Although the serious-minded Miss Leslie scorns the mufti-clad Astaire as a wartime shirker, for reasons known only to the scenarists Astaire refuses to inform her of his gallant airborne exploits. Naturally this imperils their romance until she inadvertently learns the truth and tearfully bids him farewell as his plane bears Astaire off to the South Pacific. Without much help from director Edward H. Griffith, Astaire glides through this airy narrative with his usual offhanded grace.

Nonetheless, even Astaire's professionalism fails to disguise the fact that he and Leslie are simply too disparate in temperament to imbue this romance with any real warmth or conviction. Barely eighteen when the film was released, Leslie epitomized the kind of steadfast, homogenized niceness that every GI supposedly dreamed of returning home to, but even here Astaire is hardly the average American buck private, no matter how hard he tries. Although she makes an ardent stab at grown-up sophistication for the occasion, Leslie's adolescent callowness makes an uneasy match with Astaire's smooth maturity. Together they essay two duets, a romantic turn to Arlen's lovely "My Shining Hour" and a breezy Stage Door Canteen jitterbug, but the result is tepid. Although she worked arduously to get the steps right, Leslie lacks the womanly grace needed to conjure up the requisite magnetism with Astaire.

Once more Astaire has to rely entirely on his own powers to make any imprint on *The Sky's the Limit*. For once he uses his limber legs as an outlet for frustration and despair instead of the usual exhilaration. Blearily intoning the brooding "One for My Baby (and One More For the Road)," he dashes glasses to oblivion with his hands and shoes, before hurling a stool at his own image reflected in a night-club mirror. The frenzied sadness of this routine seems way out of proportion to the plot incident that prompts it. Perhaps Astaire was really directing his rage at all the undistinguished material he had been handed lately.

Fortunately for Astaire, an exciting musical era was beginning across town at MGM, and Arthur Freed, the man largely responsible for it, very much wanted Astaire to contribute. An ex-songwriter turned producer, Freed's greatest gift was his remarkable instinct for searching out talent and mounting it properly, plus his willingness to take risks with the artists he trusted. Practically every memorable MGM musical for the subsequent fifteen years bore his imprint; performers like Gene Kelly, Cyd Charisse, and Judy Garland achieved their greatest triumphs under his supervision, while directors Vincente Minnelli, Stanley Donen, and Charles Walters literally owed their careers in movies to Freed's encouragement. Perceiving that Astaire was stagnating as a freelance performer, Freed offered

ZIEGFELD FOLLIES (1946). With Lucille Bremer in the "Limehouse Blues" segment

*ZIEGFELD FOLLIES (1946). With Gene Kelly in
"The Babbitt and the Bromide"*

him a long-term contract and a rejuvenated future at MGM: by the end of the decade, this promise was more than amply fulfilled.

Astaire's first assignment under the new regime was *Ziegfeld Follies* (made in 1944, released in 1946), MGM's opulent tribute to the patron saint of the splendiferous revue. Under the benign supervision of William Powell on Ziegfeld's perch in Metro's pink-clouded sound-stage Paradise, the *Follies* prodigally overflows with Technicolored swash and starry cameos culled from the MGM talent roster. Its varied diversions range from Fanny Brice to *La Traviata*, from Lena Horne undulating about the vicissitudes of passion in steamy climes to Judy Garland parodying a Greer-Garsonish dramatic diva who wants to forsake biography for cheesecake. It's all faintly ponderous and at times more than a little foolish, but there's no denying the film's eye-popping audacity and style.

As a welcoming gesture to the newest addition to the ranks, Astaire is given four numbers to everyone else's one. Prophetically brushing shoulders with Cyd Charisse in tutu during the opening "Bring On the Beautiful Girls," Astaire returns for two story ballets with haughtily graceful Lucille Bremer. "This Heart of Mine" evokes the haunting specter of "Let's Face the Music and Dance"

from *Follow the Fleet*, with its thread of narrative about a party-crashing jewel thief whose yearnings for Bremer overcome the lure of her diamonds. The number is filmed in intriguing fashion; rather than photographing this dance drama straight-on against a theatrical backdrop (as was done in *Follow the Fleet*), director Minnelli envelops Astaire in a dizzying three-dimensional swirl of color, props, and sweeping camera movements.

The process is repeated for an Astaire-Bremer foray into the somber exoticism of "Limehouse Blues." As an ill-destined coolie skulking through the fogbound London slum set left over from *The Picture of Dorian Gray*, Astaire dreams of romancing Bremer amidst an hallucination of "Chinese" décor, before expiring from a random gunshot intended for a pair of storebreaking thugs. The setting, the song, even the notion of Astaire done up as an ersatz Oriental seem hopelessly tasteless and kitschy, yet Astaire redeems the number by performing the cartwheeling, fan-flicking fantasy sequence with superb panache and altering his usually animated features into a mask of mute longing. His refusal to satirize the material forges something genuinely moving out of a cardboard concept.

Less startling but of greater note to posterity is his first and only screen meeting with rival dancing ace Gene Kelly for "The Babbitt and the Bromide," a number which Astaire and his sister had triumphantly introduced a generation earlier in *Funny Face*. This vignette might have been really intriguing if it had chosen to contrast Kelly and Astaire's choreographic differences, pitting Kelly's muscular acrobatics against Astaire's weightless agility. Instead they merge styles for a spree of slap-stick frivolity and light-hearted tap one-upmanship, which is nonetheless engaging.

Before he trekked to Hollywood, Minnelli's striking innovations with scenic tints and textures had startled Broadway. Astaire's color debut in *Ziegfeld Follies* gave Minnelli the chance to run riot with his palette to dazzling effect, although Minnelli's obsession with décor occasionally overwhelmed the material it served to illustrate. Assigned to direct Astaire in *Yolanda and the Thief*, Minnelli bravely charged over the edge into pure Technicolor phantasmagoria, to the bemused admiration of a knowing coterie and the bafflement of the mass audience.

Yolanda and the Thief (1945) has nothing if not remarkable daring. Unlike most musicals, it doesn't pretend to have even a tenuous connection to the real world—its stylized characters inhabit a vivid-hued never-never land to tell a story of the purest whimsy. Yet for all the novelty of its aspirations, *Yolanda* sadly misfires in execution. The incredible plot, concerning an American con man who tries to bilk a convent-bred Latin heiress of her millions by posing as her guardian angel, has an arch, cloying flavor. Yolanda's misguided credulity would have seemed insipid under any conditions, but the error was compounded by casting Lucille Bremer in the part. Perhaps a wistful gamine like the Leslie Caron of the fifties could have mimed steadfast belief in Yolanda's good fairy convincingly, but the frosty Bremer is much too worldly and mature to bring it off. Furthermore Astaire's remorseless extortionist is an extremely unpleasant character, who patronizingly harangues the ingénue while preying on her innocence and religious devotion.

Worst of all, this purported musical fantasy is remarkably stingy in the song-and-dance department. Astaire's most ambitious number is a modish surrealistic dream ballet, supposedly symbolizing the conflict between Lucille and lucre. It begins promisingly as Astaire wanders from the heightened unreality of the movie's village square into the stark, Daliesque landscape of his perturbed psyche, but the number eventually collapses under the weight of its pretentious imagery and mannered choreography. His

YOLANDA AND THE THIEF (1945). With Lucille Bremer

"Coffee Time" duet with Bremer is infinitely more winning; significantly it's not about anything whatsoever, except the sheer joy of movement and music. A hand-clapping, Latin-accented jitterbug, the number recaptures the spontaneous élan Fred had once had in such Rogers-partnered production numbers as "The Continental," heightened by Minnelli's dazzling white, yellow, and brown color scheme.

Yolanda's crooked pursuer is quite the most unsavory part Astaire had ever tackled. In a persuasive imitation of underworld nastiness, Astaire subdues his usual ebullience, lowers his voice to a raf-

fish monotone and cynically rations his charm to the moments when he's trying to put one over on the gullible Lucille. Although the combination was a bit too acrid here, Yolanda's thief provided the rough outlines for a persona that Astaire returned to often in years to come —the slightly dour skeptic resigned to his solitary world until some spirited heroine lures him out of his introversion. *Yolanda*'s failure disheartened Astaire and dashed Lucille Bremer's hopes for major stardom, but its hothouse flamboyance served an important purpose: both Minnelli and Astaire sifted out its excesses while retaining a bit of its innovative spirit for their respective later projects.

In the meantime, with *Ziegfeld Follies* still awaiting a definite release date, Astaire had to face the consequences of his second successive popular failure. Determined to be associated with a hit, Astaire took the logical but unfortunate step of returning to Paramount for another turn with Crosby. Astaire got what he ostensibly wanted—*Blue Skies* (1946) turned out to be the highest-grossing film of his career to date—but one wonders whether the price he had to pay for this was worth it. While Crosby had overshadowed Astaire in *Holiday Inn*, in *Blue Skies* he overwhelms him completely. Allotted even less footage than leading lady Joan Caulfield, Astaire is relegated to the thankless role of narrator and innocuous pal to Crosby, pining hopelessly for Caulfield and disappearing for reels at a time while Bing dispenses with the romantic interest and the lion's share of the songs.

Astaire not only lacks a partner of his own to dance with, but the powers behind *Blue Skies* hardly allow him to dance at all. When he does dare to do so, the film callously polishes Astaire off by having him topple off a platform in the midst of a routine, thanks to booze and unrequited passion. This waste of his talents might have been more tolerable had the rest of *Blue Skies* been as unpretentious and diverting as its Crosby-Berlin predecessor.

YOLANDA AND THE THIEF (1945). With Lucille Bremer and Jane Green

BLUE SKIES (1946). With Bing Crosby

BLUE SKIES (1946). With Olga San Juan (at Fred's right)

However, under the pedestrian direction of Stuart Heisler (a last-minute replacement for Mark Sandrich, who died suddenly just before production began), *Blue Skies* rambles interminably through a heavy-handed quarter-century cavalcade of Berlin standards soldered to a tedious misalliance between homebody Caulfield and Crosby, an itchy-footed singer-maitre d' who goes through night clubs like Kleenex. Crosby's patented casualness sinks into droopy-lidded lethargy under the circumstances, while Caulfield has all the allure of a Breck ad in motion as the girl whom both Crosby and Astaire find so intoxicating.

Apart from one sprightly vaudeville shtick with Crosby, Astaire's only moment of glory in *Blue Skies* is "Puttin' On the Ritz," the conscious apotheosis of his inimitable style. Garbed once more in tails, he builds slowly into a breath-taking display of grace and speed as he vehemently beats his curve-handled cane in crashing syncopation to his tap motifs. This virtuoso display turns faintly surreal as he parts a curtain and a mirrored door to reveal ten miniature Astaires in the background whirling in counterpoint to the triumphant dervish in close-up. A brilliant summation of his blazing technique and unique brand of elegance, this number was intended by Astaire to be a kind of valedictory farewell; in 1946 he announced his firm decision to retire from the screen.

Astaire had always threatened to halt as soon as his work began to stale, but what had really happened was that while his prowess remained undimmed, by the forties his style no longer matched the contemporary mood. With Gene Kelly now garnering the admiration that had greeted his work ten years earlier, Astaire could have persevered as a second-rate star perennially in support of the likes of Bing Crosby, but such prospects were hardly appetizing. So, with typical tact Astaire chose to withdraw with a debonair bow.

During his two years of self-imposed exile from the screen, Astaire was anything but inactive. Apart from inaugurating the first franchise in a nationwide chain of Fred Astaire dance studios, he finally had the time to devote to a consuming interest in breeding race horses. Yet the habits of forty years in the limelight proved harder to sever than Astaire had anticipated. Just as he began casting around for a graceful way to announce his readiness to return to work, the fates stole a page from the hoariest of all movie-musical scenario clichés: Gene Kelly had just fractured an ankle during rehearsals for *Easter Parade*, and MGM was in desperate need of someone to sing and dance opposite Judy Garland. The someone turned out to be Fred Astaire, and the impromptu *Easter Parade* (1948) turned out to be Astaire's most entrancing movie since *Swing Time*.

Another nostalgic foray through Irving Berlin's lush garden of verses, *Easter Parade* bears a superficial resemblance to *Blue Skies* —but what a difference the right combination of talent and intelligence makes. Unlike its equivalent at Paramount, *Easter Parade* is a movie of consummate craftsmanship, gorgeously mounted and adroitly tailored to take full advantage of its performers' gifts. After so many frustrating false starts throughout the forties, *Easter*

THAT'S ENTERTAINMENT

Parade finally showcases Astaire's versatility in unstinting measure. Alone he runs amok amidst the drums in a toy store, or gyrates sinuously in slow motion to "Steppin' Out With My Baby"; with the painfully chic Ann Miller he swirls with stately elegance while reminding her, "It Only Happens When I Dance With You." Yet he quickly changes his tune for a speedier tempo when he comes up against Garland's dynamic drive, shedding his aristocratic airs for a gleefully hokey "When the Midnight Choochoo Leaves for Alabam'" before putting them back on again as the pinky-raised, gap-toothed "A Couple of Swells" with the infectiously antic Judy. While none of these routines individually constitutes an Astaire peak, the effect of such consistent brilliance is far more satisfying than the isolated great moments of *Broadway Melody* and the like.

The Frances Goodrich-Albert Hackett-Sidney Sheldon screenplay so thoroughly suits Astaire that it seems impossible that it wasn't written with him in mind in the first place. There is an air of déjà vu as Astaire, playing a Taft-era vaudeville dancer, is informed by his haughtily indignant partner Ann Miller that "There's no future in my being just a ballroom dancer,"

EASTER PARADE (1948).
With Judy Garland

and that she intends to ditch him to do a solo. At this point the plot deviates from biography into fiction as Astaire picks Garland at random out of a beer-joint chorus line, myopically determined to turn her into a carbon-copy facsimile of La Miller. When Garland reveals her own staggering gifts to an ecstatic Astaire, he trades in his dancing tails for trampish rags, and they rise meteorically from vaudeville to Broadway while Miller twitches with pique.

The bare outlines of this backstage yarn seem standard enough, but under Charles Walters' unobtrusive but polished direction,

Easter Parade embroiders it with unusual poignance. For all its gaudy production values, the film has a touchingly intimate feel to it. Astaire's character has a darker side to it than usual, which parallels and draws its conviction from Astaire's own complexities. In *Easter Parade,* he plays a performer so immersed in his work that he is impervious to emotion —his tireless professionalism renders him obtuse when he has to deal with Garland as a woman rather than a fellow hoofer. "You're nothing but a pair of dancing shoes," the smitten Garland shrieks with frustration, and she is right—until her bluntness jolts him into trusting his feelings rather than his reflexes. Now nearly fifty and never the most sensual of actors, Astaire is utterly convincing as a man who almost has to be coaxed into love, and he bridges the transition between indifference and tenderness with assurance and conviction.

But it is really Garland, the most talented co-star he ever had, who provides the spark that makes their relationship so convincing. Her unstable health caused numerous production delays, and the strain shows in her appearance, which fluctuates wildly from scene to scene. Yet apart from *A Star Is Born*, this is probably Garland's most varied and moving performance. Playing a heroine temporar-

EASTER PARADE (1948). With Peter Lawford and Judy Garland

EASTER PARADE (1948). "A Couple of Swells"

THE BARKLEYS OF BROADWAY (1949). With Ginger Rogers

ily unsure of her talents and ignored in love, Garland finds a perfect vehicle to channel her haunting intensity, plus ample opportunity to display her dazzling gift for drollery. Throughout *Easter Parade*, she and Astaire seem to take boundless delight in each other's talents, and their onscreen rapport radiates a freshness that had eluded Astaire ever since Ginger had opted for Oscars instead of encores.

Easter Parade overnight reestablished Astaire as a top-rank force in the movie musical, creating a momentum that would sustain him for nearly a decade. Anxious to capitalize on this triumph, Metro concocted *The Barkleys of*

Broadway expressly to reunite Astaire and Garland. However, at the last minute, physical exhaustion and her ever-deepening emotional afflictions forced Garland to bow out. At this point, someone took another glance at the script and realized that it afforded the ideal occasion for an event Astaire aficionados had sentimentally longed for since 1939—a reteaming with Ginger.

For those people whose affection for the Astaire-Rogers alchemy borders on idolatry, *The Barkleys of Broadway* (1949) defies objective criticism. Ten years had tempered Astaire's ebullience and apparently stiffened Ginger's joints, but their interplay still conjures much more

THE BARKLEYS OF BROADWAY (1949). Josh and Dinah take a bow.

of their unique charm than anyone had a logical right to expect. *Barkleys* never quite lives up to the legend that envelops every frame of the film, but as one ignores the foibles of beloved old acquaintances, one gladly puts up with the film's flaws out of gratitude for what it still preserves. The lapses are clear: the Gershwin-Warren score can't hope to compete with the lingering memories of Kern, Gershwin, and Berlin, and many of the numbers carelessly misuse Astaire's and Rogers' gifts, whimsically dressing them in kilts for the archly Celtic "My One and Only Highland Fling," or obscuring them behind a curtain of fast-stepping choristers for the uninspired "Manhattan Downbeat" finale.

The film most defiantly challenges the ghosts of memory when Astaire and Rogers belatedly team up for the dance duet to "They Can't Take That Away From Me" that had been cruelly denied them in *Shall We Dance*. Seen through a haze of wistful nostalgia, one only realizes afterward how disappointing the moment is. In trying so blatantly to recapture the team's youthful enchantment, the number has a disconcerting archeological air to it; Astaire and Rogers still remember the steps, but they can't seem to recall the motivations for them. Their frolicsome drum-seasoned tap run-through (also

featuring a much more flatteringly gowned and photographed Rogers) is more effective because it tries for much less—here Astaire and Rogers simply try to entertain on their own present terms, rather than pit themselves against the insuperable memory of their former selves.

While the musical numbers evoke the spirit of the onscreen Astaire-Rogers teamwork of yore, the Betty Comden-Adolph Green screenplay wittily exploits the public's notions of Astaire and Rogers' allegedly tempestuous behind-the-scenes relationship. On stage, Josh and Dinah Barkley wear their crowns as the dancing royalty of Broadway with unruffled ease, but backstage Dinah bristles at the implication that he has played musical Svengali to her blindly obedient Trilby. The infuriated Dinah determines to prove her histrionic gifts alone in the loftier sphere of the Drama, while Josh scoffs at her aspirations and tries to mollify her in song with "You'd Be Hard to Replace." Comden and Green grudgingly allow Dinah to prove her point and show her mettle by impersonating Sarah Bernhardt, reciting the Gallic call-to-arms in French, no less, but the unfortunate Rogers turns the "Marseillaise" into mayonnaise with her eye-popping guttural snarlings. While Rogers emotes, supposedly to the breathless acclaim of all Broadway,

THREE LITTLE WORDS (1950). With Vera-Ellen

Astaire dips into his bottomless bag of movie wizardry with "Shoes With Wings On," as a shoe-store clerk overcome by an infinity of high-stepping Capezios scampering maniacally in all directions.

Yet apart from Ginger's histrionic mishaps, she and Astaire paradoxically most closely approximate their original incandescence in the boudoir and the dressing room, rather than swaying in center stage. Despite the intervening ten years, after nine films together Astaire and Rogers have an innate understanding of each other's verbal rhythms and mannerisms; with a sure assist from director Charles Walters, this is one movie married couple that really seems married. The self-conscious drive with which Astaire often attacked his lines dis-

appears here, as Fred and Ginger blend with and interrupt each other with a seamless intimacy that is heartwarming to witness.

Barkleys met with a delighted reception everywhere, but possibly even more gratifying was the recognition Astaire received the same year from his peers in the movie industry. In acknowledgment of his fifteen-year supremacy in the movie musical, Astaire was awarded a special honorary Oscar in 1949.

Astaire next aligned himself for the first and only time with a producer other than Arthur Freed at MGM to play opposite Red Skelton in *Three Little Words* (1950). Generally speaking, producer Jack Cummings' efforts were aimed at a rather more

THREE LITTLE WORDS (1950). "Mr. and Mrs. Hoofer At Home"

prosaic standard than Freed's, and *Three Little Words* proved no exception; although smoothly competent down to the last detail, under Richard Thorpe's anonymous direction, this film is ultimately less memorable than an uneven but innovative failure like *Yolanda and the Thief*. *Three Little Words* is basically another innocuous example of a particularly uninspiring movie subgenre—the songwriter biography. Following the tradition of blending largely fictional incidents with a songbook of the composer in question, it relates the saga of Bert Kalmar (Astaire), a vaudevillian turned lyricist when a leg injury curtails his career, and composer Harry Ruby (Skelton), whose respective avocations for magic and baseball cause endless friction in their working relationship. These desultory proceedings are frequently interrupted by a profusion of slickly mounted production numbers keyed to their songs. However, such tinkly tunes as "So Long Oolong," "I Love You So Much," and the title song don't lend themselves as readily to such comprehensive treatment as did the more sophisticated work of Gershwin, Porter, and Rodgers and Hart in their turn.

Luckily, the film also contains a host of persuasive performances which manage to lift *Three Little Words* somewhat above the ordinary. Presumably out of deference to some form of historical accuracy. Skelton remarkably subdues his usual gangling looniness, and his teaming opposite Astaire is much less jarring than might have been expected. And as the usual endlessly sage, perpetually knitting biographical spouse, Vera-Ellen contributes a very winning performance, proving an especially adept dance partner for Astaire. Together they clatter in unison in matching tails and top hats for the opening "Where Did You Get That Girl?" and glide weightlessly to Kalmar and Ruby's "Thinking of You." But the freewheeling "Mr. and Mrs. Hoofer at Home" is a particular treat, as they depict a pair of tap-happy zanies who eat, converse, bicker, and make love entirely in a jive-tempo dance and mime, clambering over furniture and smashing through walls as Fred twirls dizzyingly around the uninhibited handsprings of his lithe partner.

As the somewhat dour and obstinate Kalmar, Astaire turns in a reflective and human performance, tempering the character's abrasiveness with a slightly earthier, more colloquial version of his patented charm. It's a thoroughly professional turn in a diverting but conventional movie; although *Three Little Words* turned out to be one of Astaire's most profitable vehicles at MGM, in retrospect practically everything else he did there left a more indelible impression.

Yet even *Three Little Words* pulsates with innovation compared to the relentlessly forgettable *Let's Dance*, Astaire's second 1950 release. Why Astaire ever agreed to this Paramount loan-out is a perplexing mystery; twice before the studio had borrowed him primarily to serve as amiable foil to one of their home-nurtured stars, and with *Let's Dance* the pattern remained monotonously unbroken, with rowdy Betty Hutton supplanting Bing Crosby this time in the center spotlight.

What separates *Let's Dance* from another mediocrity like *Blue Skies* is that this one doesn't even serve as a congenial vehicle for Paramount's own attraction, much less for Astaire. In this rather moist tale, Hutton plays a war widow who sings, dances, and dispenses cigarettes in a night club while fighting to keep her five-year-old son out of the musty clutches of her imperious Brahmin grandmother-in-law. Even if it had been directed by someone more scintillating than Norman Z. McLeod, the clammy maternity evoked by the scenario couldn't be more temperamentally incompatible with the abilities of Hutton, whose trump suit is raucous egocentricity. Although the screenplay was co-written by Allan Scott, who had worked on more Astaire vehicles than any other scenarist, Astaire is not much more happily cast. He has almost nothing to work with as an old flame of Betty's, who tries to help her out of her predicament while recapturing her affections in the process. Through

LET'S DANCE (1950). With Gregory Moffett and Betty Hutton

LET'S DANCE (1950). Dancing to "Oh, Them Dudes"
with Betty Hutton

most of the film, he takes Paramount at its word, genially encouraging Hutton from the sidelines while the camera focuses on the heroine in close-up, ferociously contorting her face into paroxysms of motherly love and apprehension.

Astaire didn't get much consolation for this dreary scenario from Frank Loesser's surprisingly flavorless score, but *Let's Dance* does contain two tedium-relieving musical moments. Pianos always did bring out the syncopated pixie in Astaire, and during one spirited rehearsal routine, he gambols inside, around, and atop a gleaming baby grand and a battered upright, pausing intermittently for some loose-jointed improvisational fingerwork at the keyboard. He and Hutton briefly generate a measure of onscreen rapport in "Oh, Them Dudes", another of the comic novelties featuring Astaire behaving outlandishly in implausible

ROYAL WEDDING (1951). Defying the law of gravity

garb, a standard event since "A Couple of Swells" worked out so well in *Easter Parade*. Here the pair impersonates two raunchy, bow-legged galoots shooting up a latter-day saloon, stalking each other with great gusto and low-comedy pan-ache. Nevertheless, Astaire really should have sat this one out.

Much better tidings awaited Astaire when he returned to the home lot for *Royal Wedding* (1951). Against the backdrop of the excitement surrounding the wedding of Elizabeth II to Prince Philip a few years before, *Royal Wedding*

is like *Barkleys,* really a cleverly refurbished autobiographical essay coyly disguised as musical fiction. Like a certain renowned musical team out of the past, Tom and Ellen Bowen are Broadway's preferred brother-and-sister act, before crossing the ocean to beguile London in general and a young Anglo-Saxon nobleman (Peter Lawford) in particular. Disdainful of emotional entanglements, Astaire is the disciplined taskmaster of the duo, while sibling Jane Powell regards her onstage frolics and her pre-Lawford swarms of admirers with the same airy off-handedness. Deviating from fact for the sake of musical-comedy logic, Astaire lets down his emotional barriers for a dalliance with solemn Sarah Churchill, but since Churchill is no Moira Shearer (originally wanted for the part) and Lawford had bared his tone-deafness in *Easter Parade*, most of the film revolves around the musical byplay between brother and sister.

Although Astaire and Powell couldn't be more genetically and chronologically incongruous, they make a remarkably ingratiating pair. Co-starred with Astaire only after first-choice June Allyson became pregnant, and second-choice Judy Garland suffered another breakdown, Powell discards much of the coy chirpiness she displayed opposite the likes of Ricardo Montalban, bantering winningly with her mellow elder sibling Astaire. Moreover, she matches him step for step in their joint dance routines. Based on an actual incident that befell the Astaires during a crossing in the twenties, Astaire

ROYAL WEDDING (1951). With Jane Powell, dancing to "I Left My Hat in Haiti"

and Powell regale their fellow passengers with a gossamer ballroom turn which becomes an hilarious slapstick rout when a sudden storm turns the ship into an ocean-borne seesaw. Under less turbulent circumstances, they riotously play against type as a seedy Brooklynese blade and his voluptuous, adenoidal babe for the verbose "How Could You Believe Me When I Said I Love You When You Know I've Been a Liar All My Life"—pounding the boards with deadpan, raffish finesse, until Powell floors Astaire with an uppercut to the jaw and drags him protesting offstage.

At age fifty-two and looking nearly every minute of it, the Astaire of *Royal Wedding* is no longer the heedless romantic of the preceding decade. Until his not terribly compelling encounter with Churchill, introverted Astaire channels his energies into his work, while his more extroverted sister leads a sufficiently active social life for both of them combined. It's a particularly congenial role for Astaire, unsurprisingly so considering that it's a knowing variation on Astaire's own history. But one of *Royal Wedding*'s greatest virtues was that it gave Astaire the opportunity to prove that age had not inhibited his agility or choreographic imagination. Prompted by love and the prestidigitation of the Metro special-effects department,

Astaire whirls in a 360-degree arc over the walls and ceiling, mindboggling proof that the laws of gravity and physics can't confine him once his limbs and spirit irrepressibly combine. Astaire's other solo is much less ostentatious but equally captivating—he dexterously maneuvers a wooden coat rack into a briskly paced duet. The passing years had if anything broadened his already astonishing range as a dancer, and his work in *Royal Wedding* and most of his subsequent fifties musicals easily proved the equal of his legendary footwork from two decades before.

The Alan Jay Lerner script could have used a stronger infusion of wit, and the Lerner-Burton Lane score cops the award as Astaire's best original score in the fifties mostly by default. Still, *Royal Wedding* is an exceedingly diverting movie thanks to Astaire and his colleagues Powell and Stanley Donen, making a more than promising solo directorial debut with this film.

Arthur Freed had tried to persuade Astaire to make *The Belle of New York* ever since the midforties; they finally got around to this project in 1952, and the result causes one to ponder the reasons why Freed was so insistent, or why in fact Astaire capitulated at all. Despite the presence of Vera-Ellen and such droll types as Marjorie Main, Alice Pearce, and Keenan

THE BELLE OF NEW YORK (1952). With Vera-Ellen

Wynn (playing his third pal to Astaire in two years) before the cameras, and the usually reliable Charles Walters behind the scenes, *The Belle of New York* founders in its own leaden fancifulness.

Derived loosely from a turn-of-he-century musical play of the same name, the film's slender romance between a fetching evangelist and a Gay Nineties sybarite was a rather threadbare premise to begin with, rendered even more lifeless by the listless dialogue and Walters' monotonous and static long takes. In an attempt to add a patina of novelty to the story, *Belle* takes Astaire's dancing-on-the-ceiling-routine in *Royal Wedding* one step further and proceeds to build the movie around it. Love literally makes Astaire and Vera-Ellen "walk on air," and they spend an inordinate amount of the movie picking their way through the clouds above the movie's lavish re-creation of Little Old New York. This was a catastrophic error of judgment on somebody's part—what had been a clever gimmick for one five-minute routine turns into a painfully arch conceit when called upon to sustain an entire movie. In *The Belle of New*

THE BELLE OF NEW YORK (1952). With Vera-Ellen

York the actors appear as unconvinced by all this as the audience, which perhaps explains why the whole film gives off a peculiarly ghostly, uninhabited quality.

Astaire's role closely resembles the one which had brought him disaster on Broadway in *Smiles*, and the passage of twenty years hadn't

made it any more appropriate. He is both too mature and much too guileless temperamentally to convince as even a reformed rake living off his aunt's reluctant largesse, and Astaire's performance here is probably his least persuasive of the decade. What makes this particularly unfortunate is that *Belle* contains some of Astaire's most superlative dancing, regrettably marred by an overindulgence in special effects. Astaire has some engaging moments cavorting with pigeons and flagpoles atop Washington Square Arch, but the too obvious reliance on double-exposures and process shots takes all the spontaneous fun out of it. Similarly, Astaire and Vera-Ellen's frolic through a horse-drawn trolley is perfectly pleasant until they gimmick it up by dancing on top of the hapless animal's back. Together they glide gracefully through some pretty tableaux for a longish Currier and Ives sequence, but Astaire's one really effective number here is his least pretentious by far—spotlighted alone on a bare stage singing and performing a subdued soft shoe to "I Want to Be a Dancing Man (with Footsteps on the Sand of Rhythm and Rhyme)." But lovely as it is, it's too little and too late to save *The Belle of New York* from its endlessly coy devices.

Fortunately, Astaire followed up this fiasco with *The Band Wagon* (1953) a genuine landmark in the movie musical and arguably Astaire's most satisfying film ever. The apotheosis of the backstage musical, *The Band Wagon* doesn't have a single discordant element,

THE BAND WAGON (1953). Tony Hunter and the cast discuss the show.

*THE BAND WAGON (1953). The "Triplets" number,
with Nanette Fabray and Jack Buchanan*

combining a cornucopia of melodic Howard Dietz-Arthur Schwartz songs, a witty and perceptive screenplay by Betty Comden and Adolph Green, Vincente Minnelli's most stylish and incisive direction, and a remarkably adroit array of leading players in a seamless collaboration. And not the least of its virtues was the fact that, once more straddling the boundary between fiction and semibiography, *The Band Wagon* gave Astaire the most complex and challenging role he was ever to find.

On the surface the plot couldn't have been more unprepossessing; a passé movie hoofer (Astaire), a lofty ballerina (Cyd Charisse), a breezy married writing team (Oscar Levant and Nanette Fabray), and a quadruple-threat impresario/director with limitless talent and even more flamboyant ego (Jack Buchanan) incongruously join forces to produce a musical. Along the way egos clash resoundingly as the forces of light-hearted diversion (Astaire) give way to arty pomposity (Buchanan), and the show founders on the road, to the accompaniment of frayed nerves and soured relationships. Ultimately, out of devotion to a common cause,

THE BAND WAGON (1953). "The Girl Hunt" ballet, with
Cyd Charisse

these dissonant personalities collaborate to create the predictable smash hit at fade-out.

What separates *The Band Wagon* from all its predecessors is the fact that Comden, Green, and Minnelli know this milieu intimately and care about it passionately, all of which makes all those limp show-must-go-on clichés resound with a vitality and conviction they never had before. Very much like their creators, these characters live in an hermetically sealed universe bounded by the walls of their métier. Darting past the pallid real world on trains linking one theater to another, Astaire, Charisse, and the rest don't know anybody except other theater people, and their relationships with each other, however personal, hinge entirely on whether or not they work smoothly together—which is why Astaire doesn't feel any personal affection for Charisse until he discovers that their approach to dance isn't so different after all. At the end of the movie, Charisse even defines her love for Astaire in terms of the long run they anticipate for the show that has brought them together.

As they had done for *The Barkleys of Broadway,* Comden

DADDY LONG LEGS (1955). With Leslie Caron

DADDY LONG LEGS (1955). A dream sequence with Leslie Caron

and Green sketch many of their fictional characters along the loose outlines of real-life prototypes; the scene-stealing Jack Buchanan character is sort of an unholy cross between Noel Coward and Orson Welles, while Levant and Fabray serve as undisguised stand-ins for Comden and Green themselves. But these inside show-biz derivations mainly serve as a witty frame of reference for the affectionate but trenchant homage to Astaire at the film's core. Intermingling exaggerated details from Astaire's history and poignantly observed facets of the onscreen myth, *The Band Wagon* both perpetuates the legend of Astaire and comments on

it as well. "Tony Hunter" is really Josh Barkley without Dinah, or Tom Bowen cast adrift in a world which no longer cares about his talents. Having tapdanced into oblivion without noticing that the world and the movies had moved on to a different tempo, Hunter has lost more than his livelihood—he has lost the central focus of his life.

The fancy-free youth of *Top Hat* had joyously vented his desire for "No strings, no connections / No ties to my affections," and twenty years later Tony Hunter has to ruefully pay the consequences. He takes his solitude philosophically, because he's not sure he could cope with anything else, or is personally

FUNNY FACE (1957). With Kay Thompson

worthy of anyone's love—but he has fierce pride in his work, and he explodes with uncharacteristic rage when he feels his talents are being neglected. And once his co-workers give full rein to his gifts, everything falls into place; his career is rejuvenated at the same time that he finds a lasting partner in his ballerina turned feline hoofer.

Practically all of the great Minnelli musicals have a bittersweet pensiveness underneath the effervescent swirl of songs and decor, and under his masterly guidance Astaire gives the most reflective and subtle performance of his life. From his nervous, unconvincing ramblings about the joys of bachelorhood to his emphatically vented broadside, "I am not Nijinsky! I am not Marlon Brando!" when his misguided director tries to turn him into something he's not, Astaire gives a performance of astonishing range and dimension. What's especially remarkable about his work here is its complete lack of egotism; playing a soured version of himself, referred to by Charisse as "practically a historical figure by now," Astaire makes Tony Hunter so compelling by refusing to color his performance with pathos or self-pity.

"We're from two different worlds, two eras, yet we're supposed to dance together," sighs Tony to ballerina Gaby, and one of the joys of *The Band Wagon* is the brilliance with which Astaire and Charisse do indeed transcend their own differences. Very much the product of the sinuous, Americanized ballet tradition which Gene Kelly epitomized, Charisse tempers her formidable sensuality with a lyrical grace which unexpectedly complements Astaire's. Their sumptuous "Dancing in the Dark" duet evokes the Astaire of old with an added Charisse fillip of stylized earthiness, while Astaire brings a caustic note of no-nonsense satire to the steamy solemnity of Charisse's undulations in the peerless "Girl Hunt Ballet." On the surface a witty send-up of *macho* Mickey Spillane's tough, lusty pulp fiction, underneath, "Girl Hunt" is really a sly pastiche of those achingly serious Gene Kelly ballets which some esthetes felt had exalted the musical into the realm of Art. As choreographed by Kelly compatriot Michael Kidd, Astaire stalks his comic-strip urban turf, and clutches the languorous Cyd with the agony of true lust while she envelops him in yard after yard of black-stockinged gam. The one thing that differentiates this number from

Kelly's "Broadway Melody" in *Singin' in the Rain* is that this one knows perfectly well how hilarious it is.

When joined by Levant, Fabray, or Buchanan, Astaire reasserts his own brand of unpretentious gaiety—often to tunes he had introduced in the original stage *Band Wagon* twenty years before —gleefully toddling with Buchanan and Fabray as squalling, fratricidal "Triplets," partnering Buchanan for the airy grandeur of "I Guess I'll Have to Change My Plan", and most delectably, clambering with his colleagues over the backstage debris for Dietz's and Schwartz' anything-goes show biz anthem, "That's Entertainment."

But rollicking as much of it is, *The Band Wagon*'s most indelible

FUNNY FACE (1957). With Audrey Hepburn

moment is one of its quietest: Astaire striding with jaunty stoicism along a train platform, softly murmuring his determination to "build a world of my own; no one knows better than I myself, I'm by myself, alone."

Tragically, the grim prophecy of this lyric soon fulfilled itself in Astaire's personal life, for after a six-month struggle Phyllis Astaire died of cancer in September of 1954. Months before, Astaire had signed with Twentieth Century-Fox for *Daddy Long Legs,* and a month after her death Astaire plunged fervently into this project in the hopes of distracting himself briefly from his loss.

Somehow, none of his anguish intrudes into the gossamer *Daddy Long Legs* at all. This ancient whimsy about a piquant orphan's infatuation with her middle-aged benefactor had been filmed twice before with Mary Pickford and Janet Gaynor, and refurbished in modern dress, DeLuxe Color and CinemaScope as a vehicle for Leslie Caron, this fairy tale retained a remarkable amount of its original archaic charm. Ever since *Lili,* Caron had been Hollywood's chief purveyor of gauche incandescence, and her wistful girlishness blends smoothly with Astaire's affable maturity, while Fred Clark and Thelma Ritter bob into view from time to time to contribute a welcome astringent note to these potentially gooey proceedings.

In *Daddy Long Legs* Astaire plays an unpretentious American plutocrat who would much rather beat his jazz drums or play musical continents than bother himself with the tedious details of high finance. Reluctant as always to commit himself emotionally, Astaire is much slower on the erotic uptake than the heroine, complicated by the fact that as her literal surrogate father he finds the notion of romance with Caron intellectually incongruous, if subconsciously appealing.

Usually any such dilemmas evaporate when Astaire and his co-star succumb to a song, and *Daddy Long Legs* provides two ostensibly ecstatic duets for that purpose. Yet strangely enough something goes intangibly awry whenever Astaire and Caron dance together; their bodies aren't really compatible, Caron seeming rather massive and thick-waisted next to Astaire, and her *en pointe* interpolations don't blend well with his ballroom-style gliding. Caron, too, had pirouetted with Gene Kelly in dreamballetland, and *Daddy Long Legs* showcases her in two sequences of this sort, rather ponderously staged by Roland Petit. Astaire figures in the first in various guises, including her guardian angel à la *Yolanda and the Thief,* and appears only fleetingly in the second, looking rather uncomfortable amidst Petit's

FUNNY FACE (1957). With Audrey Hepburn

gaudy, earnest pretensions. They fare better together in the parodistic "Sluefoot" rock-and-roll routine, but Astaire and Caron's rapport only emanates any real sparkle during the smoothly crafted romantic stretches between songs. These moments and Astaire's disarming version of Johnny Mercer's "Something's Gotta Give" were assets enough to make *Daddy Long Legs* a pleasant interlude in the careers of both stars.

More determined than ever to keep working, Astaire next agreed to play his first father role in *Papa's Delicate Condition* for Paramount, but Audrey Hepburn and *Funny Face* intervened. Produced by Arthur Freed's long-time assistant Roger Edens, and directed by *Royal Wedding*'s Stanley Donen, who had gone on to do *Singin' in the Rain* and *Seven Brides for Seven Brothers*, *Funny Face* even makes the pleasant *Daddy Long Legs* seem limp and pedestrian in comparison. Bursting with exuber-

SILK STOCKINGS (1957). With Cyd Charisse

ance and lyricism and saturated with the most striking blend of colors ever seen in a musical, *Funny Face* (1957) joined *The Band Wagon* at the pinnacle of Astaire's late-career achievements.

While *The Band Wagon* pitted light-hearted showmanship versus artiness as its central conflict, *Funny Face* counterpoints the elegant lure of the world of *haute couture* against the grubbier milieu of beatnik intellectualism. Considering that Astaire stands firmly on the side of the former and that Donen, the most elegant of directors, lurks behind the viewfinder, there can hardly be any doubt as to which side wins. Once more playing a variation on Pygmalion, Astaire impersonates a Richard Avedon-esque high-fashion photographer who plucks earnest sparrow Hepburn out of a dingy Greenwich

Village book shop and transforms her into a radiant swan during a junket to Paris for a magazine layout. On paper the characters don't exactly resonate with depth, and the script takes some gratuitously cheap shots at fifties bearded bohemianism, apart from implying that there must be something radically wrong with a woman who would rather think and read books than pose for glossy pictures in beautiful clothes.

Fortunately, *Funny Face* doesn't take this script at all seriously; Donen merely uses it as a springboard for an exhilarating display of gorgeous visual style and the kind of light-hearted effervescence that movie musicals perpetually strive for and practically never achieve. As befits the theme, *Funny Face* resembles a sumptuous sheaf of *Vogue* layouts miraculously set in motion, and the world it evokes is incredibly glamorous and seductive. Practically every number is keyed to a different and vivid visual motif: delirious magazine editor Kay Thompson exhorts her gullible readers to "Think Pink" and the screen explodes with pink clothes, pink toothpaste, pink shampoo, and pink people; amid the diffused red light of his darkroom Astaire sings the title song to Hepburn; later on, to "He Loves and She Loves," they swirl ecstatically amid a pastoral impressionistic landscape of blue streams and green meadows.

With *On The Town,* Donen had infused the musical with the fresh breeze of real-city locales, and *Funny Face* explores Paris with the same zest and vitality as the three principals exultantly stride through the city, greeting the startled locals with an ebullient "Bonjour Paris." In this delicious artificial universe even the most implausible events carry their own conviction, and the film concludes with one of the most intoxicatingly romantic images in all of the movies—Astaire and Hepburn swaying in an embrace to Gershwin's " 'S Wonderful" while a raft slowly bears them up a stream into infinity.

Donen's innovative camera work and vigorous pacing are matched by the vitality and élan of his three principal performers. As the eccentric, sophisticated fashion editor, Kay Thompson looks like a comic-strip Modigliani and lustily devours every scene she is in. Appropriately, Hepburn seems the product of a different species altogether, all tremulous sincerity and elfin im-

SILK STOCKINGS (1957). With Cyd Charisse, Joseph Buloff, Jules Munshin, and Peter Lorre

pulsiveness. Framed by Donen's loving *mise-en-scène,* she also makes a limber and vital partner for Astaire. It's doubtful that audiences in the fifties were really disturbed by the disparity in their ages, inured as they were to seeing her gazing ardently into the eyes of such elder statesmen of the screen as Humphrey Bogart and Gary Cooper. As for Astaire, this is one of his gentlest, most low-keyed performances, despite a few pointed Ugly-American gaucheries aimed at existentialists and other such pretentious riffraff. In customary style, he tackles one energetic solo in which he transforms his raincoat and umbrella into the paraphernalia of a swirling imaginary bullfight, and he delivers a twangy, jubilant rendition of "Clap Yo' Hands" with the brass-lunged Thompson. However, Astaire spends most of the movie delicately awakening Hepburn's senses; at nearly sixty his subtle gallantry still transcends the wear of time that marks his face.

During the fifties Hollywood desperately tried to recoup its dwindling audiences and evoke its halcyon past through a series of misbegotten remakes of earlier triumphs. In 1956, MGM had already given *The Women* a facelift as *The Opposite Sex* and turned *The Philadelphia Story* into *High Society,* each more anemic than the previous such attempt. Thus it was

no surprise when *Ninotchka* returned the subsequent year buried inside *Silk Stockings,* following a stopover on Broadway. Although any project that reunited Astaire with Cole Porter and Cyd Charisse automatically had its compensations, *Silk Stockings* (1957) gave Astaire a rather sobering descent from the high-flown sophistication of *Funny Face.*

Silk Stockings tries frantically to bring the champagne effervescence of the original up to date, but the result is distinctly on the flat side. In this new version, the stern female Soviet comes to Paris to wrest a Russian composer away from the materialistic grasp of an American movie producer (Astaire) and the imperialistic allure of "America's Swimming Sweetheart" (Janis Paige at her brassiest), who is slated to star as the Empress Josephine in Astaire's latest gaudy epic. Of course, the comrade herself succumbs to French finery and "the urge to merge with the splurge of the spring" that Astaire keeps reminding her of. The script burlesques the Bolsheviks with sledge-hammer subtlety, rendered cruder by the astonishingly static direction of Rouben Mamoulian. In another time Mamoulian had been renowned for the grace and fluidity of his movies, but *Silk Stockings* is remarkably ugly to look at, as the CinemaScope camera stays nailed to the floor to record actors saying witless things while caged in drab interiors.

Unsurprisingly, the performances suffer greatly under the circumstances. Astaire tries hard to ingratiate, but his breezy Yank abroad of the thirties has curdled into the Ugly American of the fifties—a bit too brash for comfort, slightly too smug in his attitudes about foreigners and women and his own allure. As for Charisse, her usual Novocaine-tinged line readings superficially suit the somber Ninotchka, but despite a noble try, the virtuosity of the role defeats her.

Yet when the two dance they miraculously become their triumphant selves once more, and the sensuality of these intervals fully communicates everything their roles. fail to convey in words. Astaire's throbbingly sung "All of You" exquisitely recaptures the charged eroticism of his "Night and Day" almost a quarter-century before. At first he taunts his repressed partner to join him by twirling with a chair instead; she hesitates, becomes intrigued, and gradually her inhibitions dissolve until before long they are sinuously clinging to each other. "Fated to Be Mated" finds them in a more athletic mood, as they course jubilantly through a deserted movie studio, bounding under a set of parallel bars, leaping from sound stage to sound stage with Charisse effortlessly perched on Astaire's hip.

However, the staggering finesse of these routines doesn't disguise the fact that Astaire and Charisse are really dancing at the wake of the musical genre that Astaire had helped create. Even such masterpieces as *Band Wagon* and *Funny Face* hadn't performed up to expectations financially, and by 1957 public favor had irrefutably shifted away from the dance musical in favor of the Rodgers and Hammerstein grandiosities on one end of the scale and the twangy gyrations of Elvis and his imitators on the other. *Silk Stockings* marked not only the end of Astaire's second great musical period, but of Charisse's film song-and-dance career as well; 1957 produced Gene Kelly's last effort in the field with *Les Girls*. Astaire accepted this cataclysm philosophically. He simply adapted his talents to television, creating several award-winning programs in which he danced with the lithe Barrie Chase. Like such colleagues as Kelly and Charisse, Astaire prolonged his screen career by accepting sporadic dramatic assignments, but this really only softened the blow. After *Silk Stockings* came and went in 1957, something cherished and special had faded from the movies forever.

Astaire interrupted his two-year absence from the screen in 1959 with a movie and a role that couldn't have been further removed from everything he had ever tackled before. *Funny Face, Royal Wedding,* and the rest had been cheerful panegyrics to love, tapdancing and Technicolor; *On the Beach* was a portentous dirge about the end of the world penned in stark black and white. A cautionary tale of the Australian survivors of a nuclear holocaust who tremble in wait for their own inevitable end, *On the Beach* epitomizes the kind of earnest seriousness that Astaire had always categorically excluded from his previous work. But times had changed, and the gravity of this movie's intentions at least reinforced the fact that even without the benefit of his dancing shoes Astaire remained a compelling screen presence.

As the rueful nuclear scientist observing the cataclysmic results of his labors, Astaire serves as the mouthpiece for director Stanley Kramer's perturbed liberalism. In the interests of fidelity to the theme, one assumes, Astaire and Kramer do everything possible to obliterate the ghost of his former blithe self from intruding into the proceedings. Harshly lit to emphasize the weary cragginess of his face, Astaire carefully pauses to weigh the significance of every word he utters, before expelling it in

NEVER GONNA DANCE

a soft, English-accented near whisper.

Thanks to Kramer's lugubrious pacing and usual simplistic preoccupation with weighty subjects, *On the Beach* now looks more like a curious sociological footnote to the fifties than the masterpiece of profound prophecy it was intended to be. Yet Kramer does persuade interesting performances from his actors, and Astaire is fully as impressive here as his co-stars Gregory Peck and Ava Gardner, for all the obvious pitfalls of their roles.

Once he had proved that he could indeed be as somber and humorless as any other character actor, Astaire returned to more familiar territory with *The Pleasure of His Company* (1961), based on a popular Broadway comedy by Samuel Taylor and Cornelia Otis Skinner. Like Taylor's other play-to-movie success *Sabrina, The Pleasure of His Company* is a slightly anachronistic mélange of epigrams and sentiment among the upper crust. Astaire plays debonair Pogo Poole, a thrice-married jet-setter and neglectful prodigal father who returns to his ex-wife Lilli Palmer's Nob Hill mansion to attend the wedding of his daughter (Debbie Reynolds) to an outspoken young

ON THE BEACH (1959). With Gregory Peck and Ava Gardner

cattleman (Tab Hunter). During his tumultuous stay, he suavely fans a few smoldering embers with Palmer, and infuriates Reynolds' fiancé by nearly persuading his dazzled daughter to chuck her matrimonial plans and join him on his pleasure-laden jaunts around the globe. He capitulates at the last minute, leaving things more or less as they were on his arrival.

The slightly antique quality of this repartee-laden bonbon is underscored by George Seaton's proscenium-arch staging, which emphasizes all the gilded talk to the exclusion of practically everything else. As a result, *The Pleasure of His Company* depends almost entirely on the charm of its cast for effect, and on that score the outcome is decidedly mixed. The role of Pogo suits Astaire admirably, and in a graceful bow-out to leading-man roles, he gives a droll and accomplished performance, tinged with the appropriate note of wistfulness. Lilli Palmer is delectable as Pogo's tempted ex-spouse; with her glistening timing and mature warmth she makes an admirable foil for Astaire. However, no

THE PLEASURE OF HIS COMPANY (1961). With Lilli Palmer

THE NOTORIOUS LANDLADY (1962). With Jack Lemmon

quirkish combination of heredity and environment could possibly explain the phenomenon of Debbie Reynolds as daughter to a pair of urbane smoothies like Palmer and Astaire. Reynolds spends at least half of her time onscreen dissolved in tears of joy, poignance, or confusion, and her perpetual soddenness has a devastating effect on the film whenever her elders aren't around. It is in talk-laden diversions like *The Pleasure of His Company* that Astaire's former dance interludes are particularly missed.

The following year Astaire reverted to the platonic second-lead status of *On the Beach* for the British-made semi-comedy, *The Notorious Landlady,* in support of Jack Lemmon and Kim Novak.

The lady in question is an American expatriate in London suspected of homicide. She rents a room to a minor lackey from the American Foreign Service (Lemon), to the horror of his superior Astaire, a stickler for protocol who doesn't want the Foreign Service tainted by scandal. Naturally, before long both Lemmon and Astaire are captivated by Novak and spend the rest of the film trying to untangle the intrigues that have blotted her reputation, so that Novak and Lemmon can return to America with her past firmly laid to rest.

Director Richard Quine meanders through this morass of blackmailers, red herrings, and Keystone Kop chases undeterred by

FINIAN'S RAINBOW (1968). With Tommy Steele

the fact that the scenario switches genre practically with every reel change. But what really subverts *The Notorious Landlady* is Novak's lassitude in the central role. As a superficially gruff and ruthless career diplomat with an untapped pool of gallantry simmering underneath, Astaire delivers a characterization much like those featured in his later song-and-dance efforts, muted slightly by the non-musical framework and the encroachment of time. Parts like this one called for a slick application of the customary Astaire brio and little else; he delivers what is expected of him quite competently, and under the circumstances he could hardly be blamed for *The Notorious Landlady*'s rather tepid flavor.

Having shifted his attention to television for his variety specials with Barrie Chase and dramatic appearances on *Dr. Kildare* and various weekly anthology series, Astaire was seen very little by audiences in the sixties. By the time he returned to the screen with *Finian's Rainbow* in 1968, musicals had returned in force if not quality, as the movie industry squandered profligate sums in quest of another overblown three-hour reserved-seat extravaganza to top the formidable grosses racked up by *The Sound of Music* and *My Fair Lady*.

As it turned out, *Finian's Rainbow* will be remembered, if at all, as Astaire's graceful, winter swan song to his earlier self, rather than as the splashy song and dance event it was intended to be. The film falls prey to most of the miscalculations that marked the abortive musical boomlet of the sixties. Overlong and maladroitly cast for the most part, its combination of Gaelic whimsies and cheery racial platitudes seemed hardly as fresh or daring in the Hollywood of 1968 compared to the Broadway of 1947. Even the lush Lane-Harburg score had lost much of its luster due to overfamiliarity and the flaccid handling it gets here. Francis Ford Coppola's direction tries to infuse some vitality into the material through his sweeping use of natural locales, but despite hordes of black and white extras streaming through meadows in a desperate facsimile of spontaneous energy, the musty aura of exhumation pervades *Finian's Rainbow*.

Yet as an unexpected epilogue to the Astaire musical saga, the film does have its fleeting pleasures; as ostensibly the most archaic presence in the film, Astaire is the freshest thing in it. As the whimsical Celt who travels to America with a pot of purloined leprechaun's gold, Astaire rather overdoes the vaudeville blarney bit, but on the

FINIAN'S RAINBOW (1968). With Barbara Hancock

*THE MIDAS RUN (1969). With Richard Crenna
and Anne Heywood*

whole he performs beautifully within the limitations of age and the lifeless surroundings. Performing a sprightly jig with screen daughter Petula Clark and a frustratingly brief angular-limbed solo, Astaire still nimbly evokes the old magic without ever straining too hard to prove he can still pass muster.

What really makes Astaire shine, however, is not so much what he does, but what he still represents. Leading a swarm of children skipping down a dusty path he remains the perennially irresistible Pied Piper, however uninspired the routine. Waving farewell at the final fadeout as he nimbly strolls off alone to greet his solo destiny, he continues to be the sprightly stoic of memory. At this stage, Astaire would have certainly been pardoned if he had chosen not to risk shattering the legend by exposing his mortality. The fact that he accepted the challenge and emerged with his dignity and the illusions of the audience intact is *Finian's Rainbow*'s one real distinction.

For all its failed aspirations it's easy to understand why Astaire would have been intrigued by the possibilities offered by *Finian's Rainbow*, but no such rationale explains why he participated in the cheesy derring-do of *The Midas Run* the following year. *The Midas Run* is the caper picture to end all caper pictures, mainly because it's so shoddily made and sophomorically conceived as to dissuade anyone from following in its shallow footsteps.

Founded on the logic that no one as dapper and ingratiating as Astaire could possibly convince as American and/or honest, the film casts him as an English secret-service official who entices Richard Crenna and Anne Heywood to join him on a scheme to hijack a shipment of gold bullion. Thanks to his devious and brilliant resources, Astaire pulls the hijack off, arranges for the government to intercept the shipment, collects his reward, and earns his cherished knighthood in the bargain.

The Midas Run has no use for any of Astaire's histrionic talents, relying on merely his elegant attitudinizing and his renowned invigorating stride to gild the film intermittently with a touch of panache.

In subsequent years, Astaire has sporadically returned to television to offer slight variations on his same *Midas Run* debonair rogue, most popularly as Robert Wagner's larcenous father in the *It Takes a Thief* series. Having cried wolf in-

THE TOWERING INFERNO (1974). As Harlee Claiborne

termittently ever since the mid-nineteen-forties, at age seventy-six Astaire no longer bothers to make any public threats to retire anymore. In fact, in the last couple of years he has been more continually active than at any time in the past decade. Nineteen seventy-four marked the first year since 1957 in which Astaire had two films in first-run release. MGM's epitaph to its former musical grandeur, *That's Entertainment!*, featured a generous sampling of Astaire routines from *Dancing Lady* through *The Band Wagon*, while the latter-day Astaire himself nimbly strode beside the dilapidated tatters of the train platform set from *The Band Wagon* to act as one of the film's narrators.

Later that year, he forsook nostalgia for that other ultra-contemporary trend, cataclysmic Sturm ünd Drang, to join an all-star line-up upstaged by the pyrotechnics of *The Towering Inferno*. Perennially the benign con man, Astaire faces the holocaust as a penniless geriatric roué who tries to charm wealthy Jennifer Jones into buying his worthless securities; yet in the crucible of disaster, affection overcomes avarice just as she topples to her demise. Astaire's role is conceived as a kind of gratuitous sentimental counterpoint to the Main Event; he dutifully exudes the requisite faded savoir-faire and strength in adversity, hampered like everyone concerned with a characterization that's merely used as cardboard kindling to stoke the flames.

In recent years Astaire has spent nearly as much time gracefully acknowledging official tributes to his legend as he has performing before the cameras. He received a Golden Globe Award and a supporting-actor Oscar nomination for *The Towering Inferno*, but although the people responsible for these accolades ostensibly honored an amiable septuagenarian with a bad case of smoke inhalation, they really had someone else in mind all the time. The pleasant elderly character actor of late is really treasured as the living remnant of the Astaire who was the most revolutionary film performer since Charles Chaplin. This Astaire would claim that he never used dance as an outlet for his emotions, but in fact, he did something much more important. When he soared in time to the rhythms of a quarter-century of musicals, Astaire channeled our joys for us and set them free on screen.

BIBLIOGRAPHY

Astaire, Fred, *Steps in Time*, New York: Harper & Brothers, 1959.

Barnett, Lincoln, "Fred Astaire", *Life* magazine, August 25, 1941.

Behlmer, Rudy, ed., *Memo from David O. Selznick*, New York: Viking Press, 1972.

Corliss, Richard, *Talking Pictures*, New York: Overlook Press, 1974.

Croce, Arlene, *The Fred Astaire & Ginger Rogers Book*, New York: Outerbridge & Lazard, 1972.

Dietz, Howard, "The Musical Band Wagon Keeps On Rollin' Along", *Look* magazine, August 18, 1953.

———. *Dancing in the Dark*, New York: Quadrangle Books, 1974.

Eustis, Morton, "Fred Astaire, the Actor-Dancer Attacks His Part", *Theatre Arts Monthly*, April, 1937.

Green, Stanley, *Ring Bells! Sing Songs!*, New Rochelle: Arlington House, 1971.

Green, Stanley, and Burt Goldblatt, *Starring Fred Astaire*, New York: Dodd, Mead & Co., 1973.

Hackl, Alfons, *Fred Astaire and His Work*, Vienna: Filmkunst, 1970.

Harvey, Stephen, "Interview with Stanley Donen", *Film Comment*, July-August, 1973.

Kobal, John, "Eleanor Powell— ..... 'I Would Rather Dance Than Eat'", *Focus on Film*, No. 19, Autumn 1974.

Lydon, Susan, "My Affaire with Fred Astaire," *Rolling Stone*, December 6, 1973.

McVay, Douglas, *The Musical Film*, New York: A. S. Barnes, 1967.

Milne, Tom, *Rouben Mamoulian*, Bloomington: Indiana University Press, 1970.

Minnelli, Vincente, with Hector Arce, *I Remember It Well*, Garden City: Doubleday & Co., 1974.

Richie, Donald, *George Stevens, An American Romantic*, New York: Museum of Modern Art, 1970.

Saltus, Carol, "The Modest Mr. Astaire Talks with Carol Saltus", *Inter/View No. 33*, June, 1973.

Spiegel, Ellen, "Fred and Ginger Meet Van Nest Polglase", *The Velvet Light Trap*, No. 10, Fall 1973.

Stearns, Marshall and Jean, *Jazz Dance, The Story of American Vernacular Dance*, New York: Macmillan, 1968.

Taylor, John Russell, and Arthur Jackson, *The Hollywood Musical*, New York: McGraw-Hill, 1971.

Thomas, Bob, *King Cohn*, New York: G. P. Putnam & Sons, 1967.

———. *Selznick*, Garden City: Doubleday & Co., 1970.

THE FILMS OF FRED ASTAIRE

The director's name follows the release date. A (c) following the release date indicates that the film was in color. Sp indicates Screenplay and b/o indicates based/on. M indicates composer(s) of the music, and L indicates the lyricist(s).

1. DANCING LADY. MGM, 1933. *Robert Z. Leonard.* Sp: Allen Rivkin and P. J. Wolfson, b/o novel by James Warner Bellah. M: Richard Rodgers, Burton Lane, Harold Adamson; L: Lorenz Hart, Jimmy McHugh, Dorothy Fields. Cast: Clark Gable, Joan Crawford, Franchot Tone, May Robson, Winnie Lightner, Robert Benchley, Nelson Eddy, The Three Stooges.

2. FLYING DOWN TO RIO. RKO Radio, 1933. *Thornton Freeland.* Sp: Cyril Hume, H. W. Hanemann, and Erwin Gelsey, b/o play by Anne Caldwell and story by Lou Brock. M: Vincent Youmans; L: Edward Eliscu and Gus Kahn. Cast: Dolores Del Rio, Gene Raymond, Raul Roulien, Ginger Rogers, Blanche Frederici, Walter Walker, Franklin Pangborn, Eric Blore, Etta Moten.

3. THE GAY DIVORCEE. RKO Radio, 1934. *Mark Sandrich.* Sp: George Marion Jr., Dorothy Yost, and Edward Kaufman, b/o play *Gay Divorce,* libretto by Dwight Taylor. M: Cole Porter, Con Conrad, Harry Revel; L: Cole Porter, Herb Magidson, Mack Gordon. Cast: Ginger Rogers, Alice Brady, Edward Everett Horton, Erik Rhodes, Eric Blore, Lillian Miles, Betty Grable, William Austin.

4. ROBERTA. RKO Radio, 1935. *William A. Seiter.* Sp: Jane Murfin, Sam Mintz, Allan Scott, Glenn Tryon, b/o play by Otto Harbach and novel *Gowns by Roberta* by Alice Duer Miller. M: Jerome Kern; L: Otto Harbach, Oscar Hammerstein II, Dorothy Fields, Jimmy McHugh. Cast: Irene Dunne, Ginger Rogers, Randolph Scott, Helen Westley, Claire Dodd, Victor Varconi, Luis Alberni. Remade as *Lovely to Look At,* MGM, 1952.

5. TOP HAT. RKO Radio, 1935. *Mark Sandrich.* Sp: Dwight Taylor and Allan Scott. M and L: Irving Berlin. Cast: Ginger Rogers, Edward Everett Horton, Erik Rhodes, Eric Blore, Helen Broderick.

6. FOLLOW THE FLEET. RKO Radio, 1936. *Mark Sandrich.* Sp: Dwight Taylor and Allan Scott, b/o play *Shore Leave* by Hubert Osborne. M and L: Irving Berlin. Cast: Ginger Rogers, Randolph Scott, Harriet Hilliard, Astrid Allwyn, Harry Beresford, Lucille Ball, Betty Grable, Joy Hodges, Jeanne Gray.

7.   SWING TIME. RKO Radio, 1936. *George Stevens*. Sp: Howard Lindsay and Allan Scott, b/o story by Erwin Gelsey. M: Jerome Kern; L: Dorothy Fields. Cast: Ginger Rogers, Victor Moore, Helen Broderick, Eric Blore, Georges Metaxa, Betty Furness, Landers Stevens.

8.   SHALL WE DANCE. RKO Radio, 1937. *Mark Sandrich*. Sp: Allan Scott, Ernest Pagano, adap. by P. J. Wolfson from story by Lee Loeb and Harold Buchman. M: George Gershwin; L: Ira Gershwin. Cast: Ginger Rogers, Edward Everett Horton, Eric Blore, Jerome Cowan, Ketti Gallian, William Brisbane, Harriet Hoctor.

9.   A DAMSEL IN DISTRESS. RKO Radio, 1937. *George Stevens*. Sp: P. G. Wodehouse, Ernest Pagano, S. K. Lauren, b/o story by Wodehouse. M: George Gershwin; L: Ira Gershwin. Cast: George Burns, Gracie Allen, Joan Fontaine, Reginald Gardiner, Ray Noble, Constance Collier, Montagu Love, Harry Watson.

10.   CAREFREE. RKO Radio, 1938. *Mark Sandrich*. Sp: Allan Scott and Ernest Pagano, b/o story by Dudley Nichols and Hagar Wilde. M and L: Irving Berlin. Cast: Ginger Rogers, Ralph Bellamy, Luella Gear, Jack Carson, Clarence Kolb, Franklin Pangborn, Walter Kingsford.

11.   THE STORY OF VERNON AND IRENE CASTLE. RKO Radio, 1939. *H. C. Potter*. Sp: Richard Sherman, Oscar Hammerstein II, and Dorothy Yost. b/o stories *My Husband* and *My Memories* by Irene Castle. M: Con Conrad, Harry Ruby; L: Bert Kalmar. Cast: Ginger Rogers, Edna May Oliver, Walter Brennan, Lew Fields, Etienne Girardot, Janet Beecher, Robert Strange, Victor Varconi.

12.   BROADWAY MELODY OF 1940. MGM, 1940. *Norman Taurog*. Sp: Leon Gordon and George Oppenheimer, b/o story by Jack McGowan and Dore Schary. M and L: Cole Porter. Cast: Eleanor Powell, George Murphy, Frank Morgan, Ian Hunter, Florence Rice, Lynne Carver.

13.   SECOND CHORUS. Paramount, 1940. *H. C. Potter*. Sp: Frank Cavett, Elaine Ryan, and Ian Hunter, b/o story by Cavett. M: Hal Borne, Artie Shaw, Bernie Hanighen; L: Johnny Mercer. Cast: Paulette Goddard, Burgess Meredith, Charles Butterworth, Artie Shaw.

14.   YOU'LL NEVER GET RICH. Columbia, 1941. *Sidney Lanfield*. Sp: Michael Fessier, Ernest Pagano. M and L: Cole Porter. Cast: Rita Hayworth, John Hubbard, Robert Benchley, Osa Massen, Frieda Inescort, Guinn Williams, Donald MacBride, Cliff Nazarro.

15.   HOLIDAY INN. Paramount, 1942. *Mark Sandrich*. Sp: Claude Binyon, adap. by Elmer Rice b/o idea by Irving Berlin. M and L: Irving Berlin. Cast: Bing Crosby, Marjorie Reynolds, Virginia Dale, Walter Abel, Louise Beavers. Remade as *White Christmas*, Paramount, 1954.

16. YOU WERE NEVER LOVELIER. Columbia, 1942. *William A. Seiter*. Sp: Michael Fessier, Ernest Pagano, and Delmer Daves, b/o story by Carlos Olivari and Sixto Pondal Rios. M: Jerome Kern; L: Johnny Mercer. Cast: Rita Hayworth, Adolphe Menjou, Xavier Cugat, Leslie Brooks, Adele Mara, Isobel Elsom, Barbara Brown, Larry Parks.

17. THE SKY'S THE LIMIT. RKO Radio, 1943. *Edward H. Griffith*. Sp: Frank Fenton and Lynn Root. M: Harold Arlen; L: Johnny Mercer. Cast: Joan Leslie, Robert Benchley, Robert Ryan, Elizabeth Patterson, Marjorie Gateson, Freddie Slack.

18. ZIEGFELD FOLLIES. MGM, 1944, released 1946(c). *Vincente Minnelli*. M: Harry Warren, Roger Edens, Douglas Furber, George Gershwin; L: Arthur Freed, Philip Braham, Ira Gershwin. Cast: Lucille Ball, Lucille Bremer, Fanny Brice, Judy Garland, Kathryn Grayson, Lena Horne, Gene Kelly, James Melton, Victor Moore, Red Skelton, Esther Williams, William Powell, Edward Arnold, Marion Bell, Cyd Charisse.

19. YOLANDA AND THE THIEF. MGM, 1945(c). *Vincente Minnelli*. Sp: Irving Brecher, b/o story by Jacques Thery and Ludwig Bemelmans. M: Harry Warren; L: Arthur Freed. Cast: Lucille Bremer, Frank Morgan, Mildred Natwick, Mary Nash, Leon Ames.

20. BLUE SKIES. Paramount, 1946(c). *Stuart Heisler*. Sp: Arthur Sheekman, adap. by Allan Scott b/o idea by Irving Berlin. M and L: Irving Berlin. Cast: Bing Crosby, Joan Caulfield, Billy DeWolfe, Olga San Juan, Mikhail Rasumny, Victoria Horne, Frank Faylen.

21. EASTER PARADE. MGM, 1948(c). *Charles Walters*. Sp: Sidney Sheldon, Frances Goodrich, and Albert Hackett, b/o story by Goodrich and Hackett. M and L: Irving Berlin. Cast: Judy Garland, Peter Lawford, Ann Miller, Jules Munshin, Clinton Sundberg, Richard Beavers, Jeni LeGon.

22. THE BARKLEYS OF BROADWAY. MGM, 1949(c). *Charles Walters*. Sp: Betty Comden and Adolph Green. M: Harry Warren; L: Ira Gershwin. Cast: Ginger Rogers, Oscar Levant, Billie Burke, Gale Robbins, Jacques François, George Zucco, Clinton Sundberg.

23. THREE LITTLE WORDS. MGM, 1950(c). *Richard Thorpe*. Sp: George Wells. M: Harry Ruby, Harry Puck; L: Bert Kalmar, Edgar Leslie. Cast: Red Skelton, Vera-Ellen, Arlene Dahl, Keenan Wynn, Gale Robbins, Gloria De Haven, Phil Regan, Debbie Reynolds, Carleton Carpenter.

24. LET'S DANCE. Paramount, 1950(c). *Norman Z. McLeod*. Sp: Allan Scott and Dane Lussier, b/o story by Maurice Zolotow. M and L: Frank Loesser. Cast: Betty Hutton, Roland Young, Ruth Warrick, Lucile Watson, Gregory Moffett, Barton MacLane, Shepperd Strudwick, Melville Cooper, Harold Huber, George Zucco.

25. ROYAL WEDDING. MGM, 1951(c). *Stanley Donen*. Sp: Alan Jay Lerner. M: Burton Lane; L: Alan Jay Lerner. Cast: Jane Powell, Peter Lawford, Sarah Churchill, Keenan Wynn, Albert Sharpe, Viola Roache.

26. THE BELLE OF NEW YORK. MGM, 1952(c). *Charles Walters*. Sp: Robert O'Brien and Irving Elinson, adap. by Chester Erskine b/o play by Hugh Morton. M: Harry Warren; L: Johnny Mercer. Cast: Vera-Ellen, Marjorie Main, Keenan Wynn, Alice Pearce, Gale Robbins, Clinton Sundberg.

27. THE BAND WAGON. MGM, 1953(c). *Vincente Minnelli*. Sp: Betty Comden and Adolph Green. M: Arthur Schwartz; L Howard Dietz. Cast: Cyd Charisse, Oscar Levant, Nanette Fabray, Jack Buchanan, James Mitchell, Robert Gist.

28. DADDY LONG LEGS. Twentieth Century-Fox, 1955(c). *Jean Negulesco*. Sp: Phoebe and Henry Ephron, b/o novel by Jean Webster. M and L: Johnny Mercer. Cast: Leslie Caron, Terry Moore, Thelma Ritter, Fred Clark, Charlotte Austin, Larry Keating, Ray Anthony. Also filmed in 1919 and 1931.

29. FUNNY FACE. Paramount, 1957(c). *Stanley Donen*. Sp: Leonard Gershe. M: George Gershwin, Roger Edens; L: Ira Gershwin, Leonard Gershe. Cast: Audrey Hepburn, Kay Thompson, Michel Auclair, Robert Flemyng, Dovima, Virginia Gibson, Suzy Parker, Ruta Lee, Sunny Harnett.

30. SILK STOCKINGS. MGM, 1957(c). *Rouben Mamoulian*. Sp: Leonard Gershe and Leonard Spigelgass, b/o play by George S. Kaufman, Leueen McGrath, and Abe Burrows, and story by Melchior Lengyel. M and L: Cole Porter. Cast: Cyd Charisse, Janis Paige, Peter Lorre, George Tobias, Jules Munshin, Joseph Buloff, Wim Sonnefeld, Barrie Chase. A musical remake of *Ninotchka* (1939).

31. ON THE BEACH. A Stanley Kramer Production, released by United Artists, 1959. *Stanley Kramer*. Sp: John Paxton, b/o novel by Nevil Shute. Cast: Gregory Peck, Ava Gardner, Anthony Perkins, Donna Anderson.

32. THE PLEASURE OF HIS COMPANY. Paramount, 1961(c). *George Seaton*. Sp: Samuel Taylor, b/o play by Taylor and Cornelia Otis Skinner. Cast: Debbie Reynolds, Lilli Palmer, Tab Hunter, Gary Merrill, Charles Ruggles, Harold Fong.

33. THE NOTORIOUS LANDLADY. Columbia, 1962. *Richard Quine*. Sp: Blake Edwards, Larry Gelbart, b/o story by Margery Sharp. Cast: Kim Novak, Jack Lemmon, Lionel Jeffries, Estelle Winwood, Maxwell Reed, Philippa Bevans, Henry Daniell.

34. FINIAN'S RAINBOW. Warner Brothers, 1968(c). *Francis Ford Coppola*. Sp: E. Y. Harburg and Fred Saidy, b/o their play. M: Burton Lane; L: E. Y. Har-

burg. Cast: Petula Clark, Tommy Steele, Don Francks, Keenan Wynn, Al Freeman Jr., Barbara Hancock, Dolph Sweet.

35. THE MIDAS RUN. Cinerama Releasing Corp., 1969(c). *Alf Kjellin.* Sp: James Buchanan and Ronald Austin, b/o story by Berne Giler. Cast: Richard Crenna, Anne Heywood, Ralph Richardson, Cesar Romero, Roddy McDowall, Adolfo Celi, Maurice Denham, John LeMesurier.

36. THAT'S ENTERTAINMENT! MGM-United Artists, 1974(c). *Jack Haley, Jr.* Sp: Jack Haley, Jr. Cast (Narration): Bing Crosby, Gene Kelly, Peter Lawford, Liza Minnelli, Donald O'Connor, Debbie Reynolds, Mickey Rooney, Frank Sinatra, James Stewart, Elizabeth Taylor.

37. THE TOWERING INFERNO. Twentieth Century-Fox-Warner Brothers, 1974(c). *John Guillermin and Irwin Allen.* Sp: Stirling Silliphant, b/o novels *The Tower* by Richard Martin Stern and *The Glass Inferno* by Thomas N. Scortia and Frank M. Robinson. Cast: Paul Newman, Steve McQueen, Faye Dunaway, William Holden, Susan Blakely, Richard Chamberlain, Jennifer Jones, O. J. Simpson, Robert Vaughn, Robert Wagner, Susan Flannery.

INDEX

ABOUT THE AUTHOR
Stephen Harvey was graduated from Stanford University in 1971 and has written for *Women's Wear Daily, Film Comment,* and the Department of Film of the Museum of Modern Art, New York, where he currently works. He is the author of *Joan Crawford,* a volume in the Pyramid Illustrated History of the Movies.

ABOUT THE EDITOR
Ted Sennett is the author of *Warner Brothers Presents*, a tribute to the great Warners films of the thirties and forties, and of *Lunatics and Lovers*, on the long-vanished but well-remembered "screwball" comedies of the past. He is also the editor of *The Movie Buff's Book* and has written about films for magazines and newspapers. He lives in New Jersey with his wife and three children.